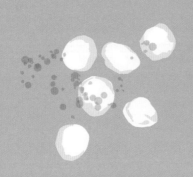

PASTA-TOPIA

60+ TWIRL-TASTIC RECIPES

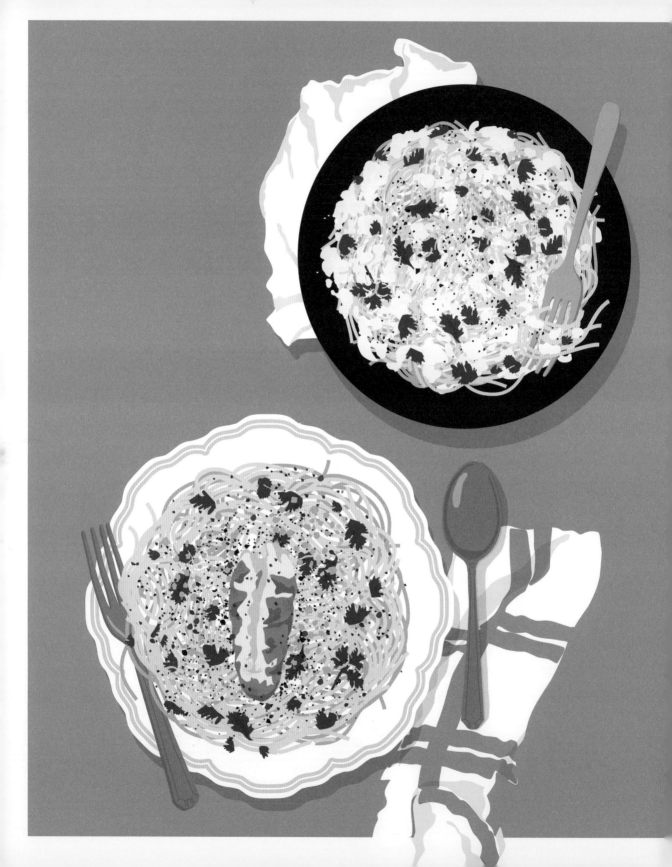

PASTA-TOPIA

DEBORAH KALOPER

ILLUSTRATIONS BY ALICE OEHR

Smith
Street
Books

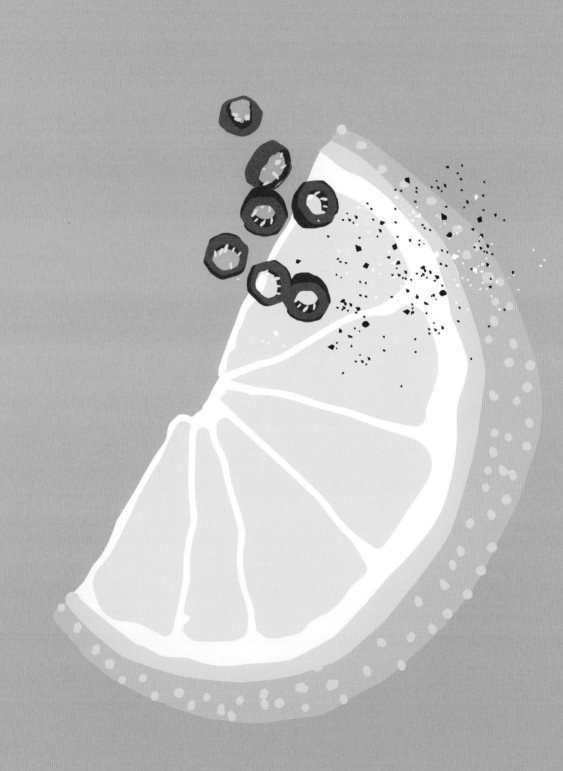

CONTENTS

INTRODUCTION

'LIFE IS A COMBINATION OF MAGIC
AND PASTA' *Federico Fellini*

Pasta actually is magic ... just two ingredients: flour
and eggs (or flour and water) mixed and kneaded
together, then rested, rolled and left to dry or
immediately cooked in a large saucepan of boiling
water to create the ultimate comfort food.

Pasta is a simple, humble dish that's also an
original 'superfood': a nourishing bowl of filling
carbohydrates deeply rooted in tradition and
culture and love, and eaten in almost every
country and by every culture around the world.

Across the ages, pasta has launched ships, helped
move Ancient armies, fuelled famished countries
and created stories of myths and legends. Although
its origins are still disputed (stories claim that the
Venetian explorer Marco Polo brought it back
from his travels in Asia in the 13th century), ancient
ruins in Italy reveal the Etruscans were making
a form of pasta in the 5th century BC. In addition,
Cato the Elder mentions a type of sweet lasagne
in 160 BC, and the first mention of ragu appears
in *Apicius*, a collection of Roman recipes written
in the 2nd century AD. From cosy family kitchens
and rustic trattorias to Michelin-starred restaurants,
pasta has made its way through history and found
its place on the world's finest elaborate menus and
on its simplest humble tables.

The anticipation of sitting down to a bowl of
delicious warming pasta, enveloped in a rich sauce
and sprinkled with parmesan is only matched by
the joyful experience and satisfaction of having
made it from beginning to end yourself, and then
sharing it with a table full of loved ones.

There is a pasta dish for every mood and occasion.
If you need a quick midweek dinner on the table in
10 minutes, then opt for traditional Cacio e pepe
(see page 45), Spaghetti aglio e olio (see page 30)
or Capellini alla checca (see page 46). Come
the weekend and the luxury of time, indulge in
slow-cooked ragus, such as Parppardelle with beef
cheek ragu (see page 53) or a handmade Pici with
duck ragu (see page 34) for the perfect long, lazy
Sunday lunch.

Today, there are more than 600 commercially
available pasta shapes with over 1300 names
(dependent on area and dialect). There's the wing-
shaped farfalle (butterfly), cupped orecchiette or
'little ears', and tiny star-shaped stellini (little stars).
There's also the macabre strozzapreti, known as
'priest stranglers', with twisted knots reminiscent of
a hangman's rope, while the beautiful long, frilled
ribbon pasta malfadine is named after a princess.

Choosing the right sauce to complement the right
pasta is a bit of an art, but with so many shapes to
choose from, every sauce has a chance to find its
perfect partner.

Small shapes, such as stellini, fregola and ditalini,
are most often served in broths and soups.

Short-cut tubes, including penne, ziti and rigatoni,
are best-suited to chunky and rustic tomato and
meat sauces that fill the hollow tubes. Short-cut
shapes that spiral and twirl, such as fusilli, trofie and
macaroni work well with pesto, cheese and cream-
based sauces, as the sauce gets caught in the twists
and turns of each shape.

Long pastas suit simple tomato sugos or oil-based
sauces, such as an aglio e olio, while hollow
bucatini can handle heartier, heavier sauces,
including amatriciana and cacio e pepe. Long,
wide, flat pasta ribbons, such as pappardelle, are
perfectly matched to rustic, hearty ragus. Thinner
ribbon pasta goes particularly well with creamy
silky sauces that coat each strand.

Finally, filled pastas only require a simple butter
or light tomato sauce to coat, allowing the inside
hidden flavour to shine through.

Whichever you choose, the pleasure of making
your own pasta is like no other in the world of
cooking. In the following pages, you'll find a
collection of traditional dishes that has something
for everyone: long pasta, short pasta, soup pasta,
filled pasta, baked pasta and even gnocchi ... is it
a pasta or not? We'll let you decide.

So get out the flour and eggs and dust down your
pasta machine. Let's make some pasta!

Buon appetito, da mangiare!

PASTA ESSENTIALS

Whether you choose to make pasta dough by hand or with a food processor, the end result will basically be the same, minus the time and elbow grease involved in handmade pasta. A food processor is quick and efficient, while using your hands allows you to understand, feel and engage with the ingredients as the dough comes to life. The choice is yours.

The ratio is always one egg per 100 g (3½ oz) of flour. You can use plain (all-purpose) flour, 'OO' flour, semolina flour or a combination of all three.

HANDMADE PASTA DOUGH

Combine the flour and salt on a lightly floured work surface. Make a well in the centre of the flour and crack in the eggs. Whisk the eggs with a fork, combining well. Gradually draw the flour from the side of the well into the eggs. Keep whisking until a soft, sticky dough starts to form.

Replace the fork with your hands and bring the dough together to form a ball. Using the heel of one hand, push the dough out and flatten it against the work surface, then fold it back onto itself. Continue to knead in this manner, dusting with flour now and again if the dough is sticky, for 10 — 12 minutes until the dough is soft, smooth and elastic. Cover with plastic wrap or place in an airtight container for 30 minutes to rest and allow the glutens in the dough to relax.

Roll the dough out and cut into your chosen pasta shape.

MACHINE-MADE PASTA DOUGH

Place the flour, eggs and salt in the bowl of a food processor and blitz until the ingredients come together and resemble small breadcrumbs. Tip the contents of the bowl onto a lightly floured work surface and form the mixture into a ball.

Knead the dough for 5 — 7 minutes, until it is soft, smooth and elastic. Cover with plastic wrap or place in an airtight container for 30 minutes to rest and allow the glutens in the dough to relax.

Roll the dough out and cut into your chosen pasta shape.

COOKING PASTA

Pasta cooking times will vary greatly depending on whether your pasta is fresh or dried, filled or shaped, thick or thin; but it all starts with a large saucepan, water and plenty of salt.

As a general rule, you want to use 1 — 1.25 litres (34 — 42 fl oz) of water for every 100 g (3½ oz) of pasta. Salting the water is essential to the final taste of every pasta recipe. Salted water flavours the pasta and determines its character before the sauce is added. While some believe that the water should be as 'salty as the sea', this is not necessarily true and should only be used as a guideline. A good ratio is usually 1½ — 2 teaspoons of fine sea salt per litre (34 fl oz/4 cups) of water.

To cook pasta, fill a large saucepan with cold water, then cover, place over high heat and bring to the boil. Add salt and return to the boil, then add the pasta and stir a few times to ensure it's not sticking together. Bring back to the boil. Cook to 'al dente', which means 'to the tooth' or 'to the bite'. This means the pasta should have some resistance when you bite into it. Some recipes require you to cook 1 — 2 minutes less than al dente. This is known as 'molto al dente' or 'slightly undercooked'. In these instances, the pasta is added to the desired sauce, where it will finish cooking and absorb the flavours of the sauce.

Sometimes a recipe will call for some of the pasta cooking water to be reserved before draining. Some chefs refer to this water as 'liquid gold', because it is slightly salty and starchy, making it great for emulsifying oil, butter and cream sauces and also for thinning out thicker tomato-based sauces.

KEY INGREDIENTS

Great pasta relies on flavourful ingredients: think artisan cheeses, extra virgin olive oils and fresh, local and heirloom vegetables. Simple, seasonal produce bursting with flavour. The Italian style of cooking known as 'cucina povera' depends entirely upon the quality of ingredients used. As a result, simplicity is key, and less is often more.

CHEESE

GRANA PADANO A hard, semi-skimmed cow's milk cheese with a grainy texture and a nutty, full-flavoured taste that's sweeter, milder and less crumbly than Parmigiano Reggiano. Produced in the Po River Valley, it is generally aged for 24 months.

PARMIGIANO REGGIANO Produced in the Parma, Reggio Emilia, Bologna, Modena and Mantua provinces, Parmigiano Reggiano is a hard cow's milk cheese with a sharp, nutty taste and savoury umami flavour. It is aged between 12 and 36 months

PECORINO ROMANO A hard, salty sheep's milk cheese produced in Lazio, Sardinia and the Tuscan province of Grosseto. Aged for 8 — 12 months, it is the star ingredient in the famous Roman dish Cacio e pepe (see page 45).

GORGONZOLA A blue-veined cow's milk cheese from the Lombardy and Piedmont regions of Italy. Gorgonzola 'Dolce', meaning sweet, has a subtle flavour with a creamy, lush texture. Gorgonzola 'Piccante' (spicy) is aged for longer, which results in bluer veins, a much stronger-pronounced flavour and a crumbly texture.

CAMBOZOLA This thick, soft, creamy cow's milk cheese from Germany is like a cross between Italian Gorgonzola and French triple cream Brie. It melts easily and is perfect for making blue-cheese sauces.

MOZZARELLA A fresh, semi-soft Italian cheese made from cow's milk with a sweet, mild, milky flavour. It's commonly added to baked pasta dishes, such as ziti and lasagne.

BUFFALO MOZZARELLA Made from the milk of water buffalos, buffalo mozzarella has a creamier, softer texture than cow's milk mozzarella and a stronger, tangier, almost sour taste, adding another dimension of flavour to pasta dishes.

BURRATA Meaning 'buttery', burrata is a ball of cow's or buffalo milk mozzarella, with a curd and cream-filled centre. Usually eaten on its own or with fresh tomatoes, basil and extra virgin olive oil, it is a decadent addition when torn, scattered or melted onto hot pasta.

BOCCONCINI Small mozzarella balls the size of small eggs. Baby bocconcini are even smaller, like quails' eggs. They are usually made from a combination of buffalo and cow's milk and are often found in pasta salads.

RICOTTA Meaning 'recooked', ricotta is an Italian fresh whey cheese. It is made from the whey left over from the production of other cheeses. Similar to cottage cheese in texture, its curds are small, creamy and sweet. Ricotta can be made from cow, sheep, buffalo or goat's milk, and each has its own distinct flavour. Layered through a lasagne or tossed through pasta, it is soft and delicious.

KEY INGREDIENTS

HERBS

BASIL Known as the king of herbs and part of the mint family, basil can lift any simple rustic tomato sauce. With its intense green colour and spicy bright herbal flavour, it is the essential ingredient in pesto Genovese (see page 87).

PARSLEY Native to the Mediterranean, parsley has been grown and used in Italian cooking since Roman times. Its herbaceous flavour complements a wide range of tomato and cream-based sauces and pairs well with vegetables, meat and seafood.

SAGE The pungent medicinal flavour of sage is transformed when simply sizzled in butter until crisp and served over gnocchi or ravioli.

ROSEMARY From the Latin 'ros marinus' meaning 'sea dew', rosemary is a robust herb best paired with gamey or rustic meat and tomato sauces.

GARLIC This member of the allium family is pungent and spicy when used raw, but mellows in flavour and aroma when sautéed or roasted. The Romans regularly used garlic in their cooking and it is a cornerstone ingredient in Southern Italian dishes, although it is used quite sparingly. Garlic clove sizes vary greatly, so use accordingly.

PANTRY

EXTRA VIRGIN OLIVE OIL VERSUS OLIVE OIL Extra virgin olive oil is made by crushing olives to a paste and pressing (or spinning in a centrifuge) the paste to extract the oil without the use of heat or chemicals. It is the 'first press' of the olives and is often labelled 'cold-pressed'. The resulting product is far superior to regular olive oil, as the absence of heat allows the oil to retain its purity of colour, aroma and flavour. Extra virgin olive oil is a brighter

green than olive oil. It has a grassy, floral taste and sometimes a peppery flavour. It must also have an acidity level below 0.08% after pressing to be classified as extra virgin olive oil.

Olive oil or pure olive oil is often a blend of olive oils containing various ratios of refined olive oil, virgin olive oil and sometimes extra virgin olive oil. It is much milder in both colour and taste.

FLOUR Pasta dough can be made with plain (all-purpose) flour, 00 flour, semolina flour or a combination of flours.

Bleached or unbleached plain flour is a multi-purpose wheat flour widely used in home cooking and baking, including cakes, breads and pastries.

00 flour is an extra-fine, soft wheat Italian flour often used for making pasta, pizza or breads. Using 00 flour results in a more-refined and delicate dough.

Semolina flour is a hard, yellow wheat flour made specifically from durum wheat. It is used to increase the strength and colour of pasta dough, as it has a heavier protein content than regular wheat flours. Orecchiette is traditionally made using only semolina flour.

TOMATOES Fresh tomatoes from your garden or a farmers' market at the height of summer will always be superior to tinned, but these are only available for a short period. So when making pasta sauces, reach for the convenience and consistency of tinned whole tomatoes.

San Marzano tomatoes are a variety of plum tomatoes grown in San Marzano sul Sarno, near Naples, and are considered to be the best and most flavoursome tomatoes for making pasta sauce.

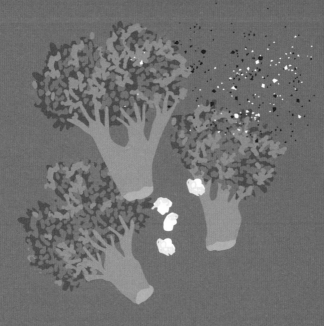

BASICS

EGG PASTA DOUGH

SERVES 4—6

400 g (14 oz) plain (all-purpose), 00 or semolina flour (or a combination of all three), plus extra for dusting and kneading

4 free-range eggs, lightly beaten

pinch of fine sea salt

Place the flour, eggs and salt in the bowl of a food processor and blitz until the ingredients come together and resemble small breadcrumbs. Tip the contents of the bowl onto a lightly floured work surface and form the mixture into a ball.

Knead the dough for 5—7 minutes until it is smooth, elastic and springy to the touch. Form the dough into a disc, wrap it in plastic wrap and set aside to rest for about 30 minutes.

On a lightly floured work surface, cut the dough into quarters, then re-wrap three of the quarters in plastic wrap.

Set your pasta machine to the widest setting and flatten the quarter portion of dough to a similar width. Feed the dough through the machine with one hand, while turning the handle with the other. Fold the dough into thirds, as if you were folding a letter, then feed the open end of the dough through the machine again on the same setting. Repeat this process 3—4 times.

Turn the dial on the pasta machine to the next thinnest setting and feed the dough through the rollers again. Continue to feed the dough through the machine, reducing the setting each time and dusting with flour if the dough starts to stick. The dough will get thinner and longer, so cut it in half to make it easier to work with.

Roll the dough to the desired thickness (this is usually the second-to-last or last setting) and immediately cut into whichever length or shape your recipe calls for. Lightly dust with flour, then pile into a loose mound and repeat with the remaining dough.

DOUGH VARIATIONS

Beetroot (beets): blitz 3 tablespoons of beetroot juice or puréed cooked beetroot with the eggs before adding the flour and salt.

Squid ink: beat 1—1½ tablespoons of squid ink with the eggs before adding the flour and salt.

Lemon: beat 2 tablespoons of lemon zest and 1½ tablespoons lemon juice with the eggs before adding the flour and salt.

EGG-RICH RAVIOLI DOUGH

MAKES ABOUT 40 RAVIOLI

150 g (5½ oz/1 cup) plain (all-purpose) flour, plus extra for dusting and kneading

165 g (6 oz/1 cup) fine semolina flour, plus extra for dusting

pinch of fine sea salt

1 free-range egg, lightly beaten

5 free-range egg yolks, lightly beaten

Place the flours and salt in the bowl of a food processor and blitz to combine. Add the eggs and 3 teaspoons water and blitz until the ingredients resemble small breadcrumbs. Tip the contents onto a lightly floured work surface and form the mixture into a ball.

Knead the dough for 5—7 minutes until it is smooth, elastic and springy to the touch. Form the dough into a disc, wrap it in plastic wrap and set aside to rest at room temperature for about 30 minutes.

On a lightly floured work surface, cut the dough into quarters. Re-wrap three of the quarters in plastic wrap.

Set your pasta machine to the widest setting and flatten the quarter portion of dough to a similar width. Feed the dough through the machine with one hand, while turning the handle with the other. Fold the dough into thirds, as if you were folding a letter, then feed the open end of the dough through the machine again on the same setting. Repeat this process 3—4 times.

Turn the dial on the pasta machine to the next thinnest setting and feed the dough through the rollers again. Continue to feed the dough through the machine, reducing the setting each time and dusting with flour if the dough starts to stick. The dough will get thinner and longer, so cut it in half to make it easier to work with. Roll the dough to the final or thinnest setting.

Trim the pasta sheet to a 64 cm x 14 cm (2 ft 1 in x 5½ in) rectangle, then cut in half lengthways so you have two 64 cm x 7 cm (2 ft 1 in x 2¾ in) rectangles.

Place 2 teaspoons of your chosen filling at 4 cm (1½ in) intervals down the middle of the dough. Lightly brush the dough around the filling with water and place the other dough strip on top. Use you index and middle fingers to press the dough down around the filling, pushing out the air and sealing the ravioli. Use a pasta crimper or sharp knife to cut out 6 cm (2½ in) squares of ravioli. Transfer to a semolina-dusted tray and cover with a tea towel..

Repeat with the remaining dough and desired filling until you have about 40 ravioli.

SEMOLINA DOUGH

SERVES 4—6

330 g (11½ oz/2 cups) fine semolina flour, plus extra for dusting and kneading

165 ml (5½ fl oz) warm water

good pinch of fine sea salt

Place the flour, warm water and salt in the bowl of a food processor and blitz until the ingredients come together and resemble small breadcrumbs. Tip the contents of the bowl onto a lightly floured work surface and form the mixture into a ball.

Knead the dough for 5—7 minutes until it is smooth, elastic and springy to the touch. Form the dough into a disc, wrap it in plastic wrap and set aside to rest at room temperature for about 30 minutes.

On a lightly floured work surface, cut the dough into quarters. Re-wrap three of the quarters in plastic wrap to ensure they don't dry out. Set up your pasta machine.

Set your pasta machine to the widest setting and flatten the portion of dough to a similar width. Feed the dough through the machine with one hand, while turning the handle with the other.

Fold the dough into thirds, as if you were folding a letter, then feed the open end of the dough through the machine again on the same setting. Repeat this process 3—4 times.

Turn the dial on the pasta machine to the next thinnest setting and feed the dough through the rollers again. Continue to feed the dough through the machine, reducing the setting each time and dusting the dough with a sprinkling of flour now and again if it is getting tacky. The dough will get thinner and longer (cut it in half to make it easier to work with, if necessary).

Roll the dough to the desired thickness (this is usually the second-to-last or last setting) and immediately cut into whichever length or shape your recipe calls for. Lightly dust with flour, then pile into a loose mound and repeat with the remaining dough.

PICI

SERVES 4 — 6

200 g (7 oz) fine semolina flour, plus extra for dusting and kneading

200 g (7 oz/1⅓ cups) plain (all-purpose) flour

1 teaspoon extra virgin olive oil

pinch of fine sea salt

Place the ingredients and 200 ml (7 fl oz) water in the bowl of a food processor and blitz until the ingredients come together and resemble small breadcrumbs. Tip the contents of the bowl onto a lightly floured work surface and knead for 4 — 5 minutes until smooth, elastic and firm, yet springy, to the touch. Form the dough into a disc, wrap in plastic wrap and allow to rest at room temperature for about 30 minutes.

On a lightly floured work surface, cut the dough into quarters. Re-wrap three of the quarters in plastic wrap to ensure they don't dry out. Using a rolling pin, roll the remaining quarter of dough until it is 2 — 3 mm (⅛ in) thick, then cut into 5 mm (¼ in) wide strips.

Using your palms, roll each strip of dough between your hand and the work surface to create long, thick and just slightly twisted noodles. They will be a little rough and uneven, but perfect for 'catching' the pasta sauce. Lightly dust with flour, then pile into a loose mound and repeat with the remaining dough.

POTATO GNOCCHI

SERVES 4—6

1 kg (2 lb 3 oz) medium floury potatoes, such as desiree or russet

1 free-range egg

good pinch of fine sea salt

200—250 g (7—9 oz) plain (all-purpose) flour, plus extra for dusting

Place the potatoes in a large saucepan, cover with water and bring to the boil over high heat. Boil for 30—40 minutes, until each potato can be easily pierced with a knife. Drain and set aside for a few minutes until cool enough to handle.

Peel the potatoes and pass them through a potato ricer, spreading the potato out on a clean work surface as you go. You can also mash them, but this can overwork the potato resulting in heavier gnocchi. Gather the potato into a mound and make a well in the centre. Add the egg and salt to the well and gently mix into the potato until just combined. Gradually add the flour, a little at a time, mixing and folding together, to form a smooth, supple dough (you may not need all of the flour). Take care not to overwork the dough or add too much flour, which will result in heavy gnocchi.

Divide the dough into six even portions. Cover five of the portions with a tea towel to prevent them from drying out. Lightly dust a work surface with flour and roll the dough portion in front of you into a 38 cm (15 inch) long rope, about 2.5—3 cm ($1-\frac{1}{4}$ in) wide. Slice the rope into 15 even pieces and set aside on a lightly floured tray. Repeat with the remaining dough.

Working in batches, cook the gnocchi in a large saucepan of salted boiling water for $1-1\frac{1}{2}$ minutes or until the gnocchi rise to the top. Strain and toss through your favourite pasta sauce.

CLASSIC TOMATO SUGO

MAKES 750 ML (25½ FL OZ/3 CUPS)

40 g (1½ oz) butter

2 tablespoons extra virgin olive oil

2 garlic cloves

100 g (3½ oz) onion, finely diced

2 x 400 g (14 oz) tins whole tomatoes

pinch of sea salt

6 basil leaves

Melt the butter and oil in a saucepan over medium — low heat. Leaving them whole, lightly smash the garlic cloves using the side of a knife, then add to the pan along with the onion. Sauté, stirring occasionally, for 7 — 8 minutes until the onion is soft and translucent.

Tip the tomatoes into a bowl and lightly crush them with your hands. Add the tomatoes, salt and basil to the pan, then reduce the heat to low and cook, stirring occasionally, for 35 — 45 minutes, until the tomatoes break down and reduce to a thick, rich sauce. At this stage, you can remove the garlic cloves and discard, or mash and stir them through the sauce.

Serve with your choice of pasta or gnocchi.

The sugo will keep in an airtight container in the fridge for 4 — 5 days.

ROASTED TOMATO SUGO

MAKES ABOUT 1 LITRE (34 FL OZ/4 CUPS)

1.5 kg (3 lb 5 oz) tomatoes, halved, cores removed

3 thyme sprigs, leaves picked

1 oregano sprig, leaves picked

2 garlic cloves, sliced

pinch of caster (superfine) sugar

sea salt and freshly cracked black pepper

3 tablespoons extra virgin olive oil

small handful of basil leaves

Preheat the oven to 170°C (340°F). Line a baking tray with baking paper.

Place the tomato halves, cut side up, on the prepared tray and scatter over the herbs, garlic and sugar. Season with salt and pepper and drizzle over the oil, then roast for 50 — 60 minutes, until soft and lightly roasted. Take care not to burn the garlic, which will result in a bitter, overpowering taste.

Remove the tray from the oven and set aside to cool slightly. Transfer the tomato and garlic to a blender and purée with the basil leaves until smooth. Taste and season with more salt and pepper if required.

Serve with your choice of pasta or gnocchi.

The sugo will keep in an airtight container in the fridge for 4 — 5 days.

BÉCHAMEL SAUCE

MAKES ABOUT 500 ML (17 FL OZ/2 CUPS)

500 ml (17 fl oz/2 cups) full-cream (whole) milk

60 g (2 oz) butter

45 g (1½ oz) plain (all-purpose) flour

¼ teaspoon freshly grated nutmeg

30 g (1 oz) finely grated fresh parmesan (optional)

good pinch of salt and ground white pepper

Warm the milk in a small saucepan over low heat.

Melt the butter in a separate saucepan over medium heat and sprinkle in the flour. Whisk the butter and flour until the mixture starts to brown and resemble the texture of wet sand. Slowly pour in the milk a little at a time, whisking constantly to avoid lumps forming. Once all the milk has been incorporated, continue to whisk and simmer for 2 — 3 minutes, until the mixture is thick and silky.

Remove the pan from the heat, whisk in the nutmeg and cheese (if using), season to taste and use immediately.

HOMEMADE 'RICOTTA' OR FRESH CURD CHEESE

MAKES ABOUT 500 G (1 LB 2 OZ/2 CUPS)

1 litre (34 fl oz/4 cups) full-cream (whole) milk

500 ml (17 fl oz/2 cups) pure cream

½ teaspoon sea salt

60 ml (2 fl oz/¼ cup) distilled vinegar

Line a large colander or sieve with muslin (cheesecloth) and set it over a bowl.

Place the milk, cream and salt in a large heavy-based saucepan and bring to the boil, stirring occasionally. Add the vinegar, then reduce the heat to a low simmer and stir for 3 — 4 minutes, until the mixture begins to curdle. Remove the pan from the heat and let it stand for 10 minutes.

Use a slotted spoon to gently transfer the curds to the lined colander and discard the remaining liquid (whey). Drain for 30 — 60 minutes, depending on how wet or dry you would like the ricotta to be.

Use immediately, or refrigerate in an airtight container for 4 — 5 days.

VEGAN 'RICOTTA'

MAKES ABOUT 500 G (1 LB 2 OZ)

300 g (10½ oz) raw cashews soaked in cold water for 4 — 6 hours or overnight, drained

2 garlic cloves, peeled

2 tablespoons lemon zest

2 tablespoons lemon juice

1½ tablespoons nutritional yeast flakes

1½ tablespoons white miso paste

1 teaspoon extra virgin olive oil

large handful of basil leaves

sea salt and freshly cracked black pepper, to taste

Place all the ingredients and 60 ml (2 fl oz/¼ cup) water in the bowl of a food processor and blitz until the mixture is well combined and resembles the texture of ricotta. Taste and adjust the seasoning, if necessary.

Store in an airtight container in the fridge for 3 — 4 days.

VEGAN 'PARMESAN'

MAKES ABOUT 150 G (5½ OZ)

55 g (2 oz/½ cup) almond meal

80 g (2¾ oz/½ cup) raw cashews

15 g (½ oz/¼ cup) nutritional yeast flakes

½ teaspoon onion powder

½ teaspoon fine sea salt

Place all the ingredients in the bowl of a food processor or high-speed blender and process to the consistency of grated cheese.

Store in an airtight container in the fridge for up to 2 weeks.

PANGRATTATO

MAKES ABOUT 100 G (3½ OZ/1 CUP)

50 g (1¾ oz) butter (see Note)

1 tablespoon extra virgin olive oil

1 — 2 garlic cloves, minced

½ teaspoon dried chilli flakes

60 g (2 oz/1 cup) panko or fine dry breadcrumbs

sea salt and freshly cracked black pepper, to taste

OPTIONAL EXTRAS

1 teaspoon lemon zest

1 teaspoon mixed dried herbs

1 tablespoon chopped mixed fresh herbs

Melt the butter and oil in a saucepan over medium heat. Add the garlic and chilli flakes and toss through for 30 seconds or until fragrant. Add the panko or breadcrumbs and any optional extras, and sauté for a further 1 minute, coating the crumbs evenly in the buttery mixture. Toast the crumbs to a light golden brown and season well with salt and pepper.

Use immediately.

NOTE:

Replace with vegan butter for a dairy-free pangrattato.

LONG PASTA

SPAGHETTI CARBONARA

SERVES 4

4 free-range egg yolks, plus 4 extra yolks to serve

1 free-range egg

125 g (4½ oz) finely grated fresh parmesan, plus extra to serve

1½ teaspoons freshly cracked black pepper, plus extra to serve

¼ teaspoon sea salt

400 g (14 oz) fresh or dried spaghetti

1 tablespoon extra virgin olive oil

150 g (5½ oz) pancetta, diced into 1 cm (½ in) cubes

chopped parsley, to serve

Whisk the egg yolks and egg, cheese, pepper and salt in a large bowl and set aside.

Cook the pasta in a large saucepan of salted boiling water until al dente. Reserve 250 ml (8½ fl oz/1 cup) of the pasta cooking water, then drain the pasta and set aside.

Meanwhile, heat the oil in a large saucepan over medium heat, add the pancetta, and cook for 5 minutes or until golden and crisp. Add the drained pasta and toss through the pancetta, coating the spaghetti in the pancetta oil. Remove from the heat.

Working quickly, pour the egg and cheese mixture into the pan and, using tongs, toss through the pasta. Add one-quarter of the reserved pasta water and toss through to melt the cheese and emulsify the egg. Keep tossing the pasta, adding more pasta cooking water, as required, to make a creamy and silky sauce that completely coats the pasta. You may only need to use up to half of the water, depending on how thick or thin you would like the sauce to be.

Divide the carbonara among four warmed pasta bowls, top with extra grated parmesan, pepper and the parsley, and finish with an egg yolk perched on top of the carbonara.

BUCATINI ALLA AMATRICIANA

SERVES 4 — 6

2 x 400 g (14 oz) tins whole tomatoes

2 tablespoons extra virgin olive oil

250 g (9 oz) guanciale, diced into 1 cm (½ in) pieces

1 teaspoon dried chilli flakes

500 g (1 lb 2 oz) fresh or dried bucatini

20 g (¾) butter

sea salt and freshly cracked black pepper

60 g (2 oz) finely grated fresh pecorino, plus extra to serve

Tip the tomatoes into a bowl and lightly crush them with your hands.

Heat the oil in a large frying pan over medium heat. Add the guanciale and cook, stirring frequently, for 7 — 8 minutes, until golden brown. Add the chilli flakes and cook for a further 1 minute, then stir in the tomatoes and cook for 12 — 15 minutes, until the sauce has reduced and thickened slightly.

Meanwhile, bring a large saucepan of salted water to the boil and cook the pasta to 1 minute less than al dente. Drain, reserving 60 ml (2 fl oz/¼ cup) of the pasta cooking water.

Just before serving, stir the butter through the sauce and season with salt and pepper, to taste. Add the pasta to the sauce and toss to coat. Add the reserved pasta water and cook for a further minute or so until the pasta is al dente. Stir through the pecorino.

Divide the pasta among warmed pasta bowls and sprinkle over a little extra pecorino.

SPAGHETTI AGLIO E OLIO

SERVES 4—6

500 g (1 lb 2 oz) fresh or dried spaghetti

200 ml (7 fl oz) extra virgin olive oil

10 garlic cloves, thinly sliced

1½ teaspoons dried chilli flakes

large handful of chopped parsley

sea salt and freshly cracked black pepper

Cook the pasta in a large saucepan of salted boiling water to 1 minute less than al dente. Reserve 250 ml (8½ fl oz/1 cup) of the pasta cooking water, then drain the pasta and set aside.

Meanwhile, place a large saucepan over low heat and add the oil and garlic. Gently cook until the garlic is just beginning to colour. Sprinkle in the chilli flakes, tossing to incorporate.

Add the drained pasta, half the parsley and the reserved pasta water to the pan. Increase the heat slightly and, using tongs, toss and turn the spaghetti through the sauce. Continue tossing and swirling the pasta around the pan for 1 — 2 minutes — the pasta water will begin to evaporate as the remaining sauce thickens and coats the spaghetti. Season to taste with salt and pepper.

Divide the pasta among warmed pasta bowls, sprinkle over the remaining parsley and serve.

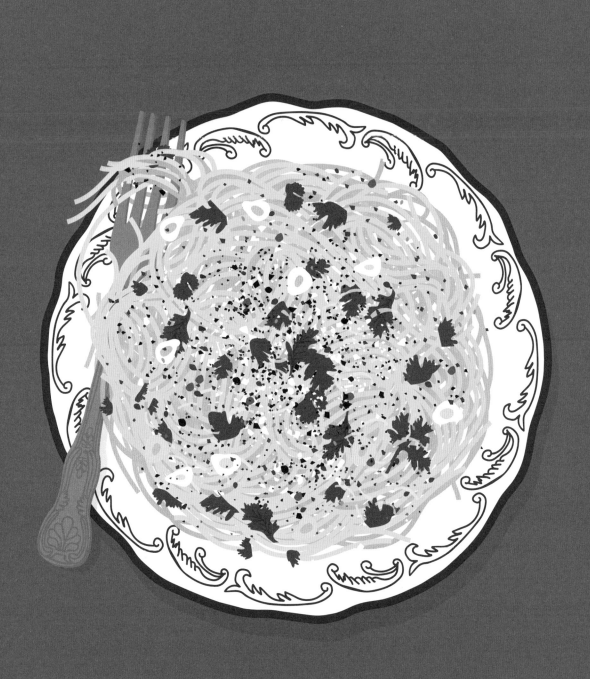

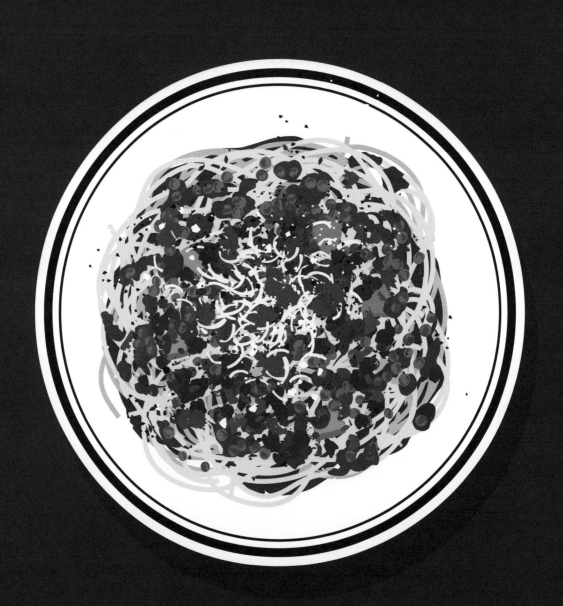

VEGAN LENTIL BOLOGNAISE

SERVES 4 — 6

3 tablespoons extra virgin olive oil

1 carrot, finely diced

1 onion, finely diced

1 celery stalk, finely diced

3 garlic cloves, minced

1 teaspoon dried basil

1 teaspoon dried oregano

pinch of dried chilli flakes

2 tablespoons tomato paste (concentrated purée)

250 ml (8½ fl oz/1 cup) white wine

2 x 400 g (14 oz) tins whole tomatoes

1 tablespoon white miso paste

1 litre (34 fl oz/4 cups) vegetable stock

300 g (10½ oz) red lentils

1 fresh or dried bay leaf

1 tablespoon red wine vinegar

sea salt and freshly cracked black pepper

500 g (1 lb 2 oz) fresh or dried spaghetti

chopped parsley leaves, to serve

Vegan 'parmesan' (see page 21), to serve

Heat the oil in a large frying pan over medium heat. Add the carrot, onion and celery and sauté for 7 — 8 minutes, until the onion is translucent and the vegetables are lightly caramelised. Add the garlic, dried herbs and chilli flakes and sauté for another 1 minute or until fragrant. Stir in the tomato paste and cook for 1 — 2 minutes, then add the wine and deglaze the pan until most of the liquid has evaporated.

Tip the tomatoes into a bowl and lightly crush them with your hands, then add to the pan along with the miso, stock, lentils and bay leaf. Bring to the boil, then reduce the heat and simmer, stirring occasionally, for 45 — 55 minutes, until the lentils are cooked through and the sauce has reduced to a bolognaise consistency. Stir through the vinegar and season to taste with salt and pepper.

Cook the spaghetti in a large saucepan of salted boiling water until al dente. Drain and toss the pasta through the sauce, completely coating the spaghetti in the bolognaise.

Divide the pasta among warm pasta bowls and top with chopped parsley and a sprinkling of vegan parmesan.

PICI WITH DUCK RAGU

SERVES 4 — 6

1 x quantity Pici (see page 17)

DUCK RAGU

10 g (⅓ oz) dried porcini mushrooms

4 x 250 g (9 oz) duck marylands

sea salt

1 carrot, finely diced

1 celery stalk, finely diced

1 onion, finely diced

½ teaspoon ground allspice

1 small rosemary sprig

1 fresh or dried bay leaf

2 thyme sprigs

2 — 3 garlic cloves, minced

170 g (6 oz) tomato paste
(concentrated purée)

300 ml (10 fl oz) red wine

1 litre (34 fl oz/4 cups) chicken stock

50 g (1¾ oz) butter

small handful of parsley, finely
chopped

1 teaspoon orange zest (optional)

freshly cracked black pepper

freshly grated parmesan, to serve

To make the duck ragu, rehydrate the porcini mushrooms in 250 ml (8½ fl oz/1 cup) hot water for 15 minutes. Strain and reserve the liquid. Roughly chop the mushrooms.

Meanwhile, season the duck with salt and place, skin side down, in a large cold frying pan. Place the pan over medium heat and sear the duck on one side for about 7 minutes or until the skin is golden brown. Turn the duck over and cook for a further 3 — 4 minutes. Remove the duck and half the rendered fat from the pan. Save this duck fat for another use, such as roasting potatoes.

Add the carrot, celery, onion, allspice and herbs to the pan and sauté for 7 — 10 minutes, until the vegetables are soft and beginning to caramelise. Add the garlic and sauté for 1 minute or until fragrant and soft, then add the porcini mushroom and stir to combine. Add the tomato paste and cook for about 4 minutes.

Increase the heat to medium — high, add the wine and deglaze the pan for 3 — 4 minutes. Add the stock and the reserved mushroom liquid and bring to the boil. Return the duck to the pan, then reduce the heat to low, cover and simmer for 2½ hours, or until the meat is falling off the bone and the sauce has reduced. Remove the duck from the pan and set aside to cool.

Remove and discard the duck skin and bones, then shred the meat into bite-sized pieces. Return the meat to the sauce and add the butter, parsley and orange zest (if using). Season to taste with salt and pepper.

Meanwhile, cook the pici in plenty of salted boiling water until al dente. Drain.

To serve, toss the duck ragu through the cooked pici. Divide among warm pasta bowls and sprinkle with freshly grated parmesan.

SPAGHETTI PUTTANESCA

SERVES 4 — 6

2 x 400 g (14 oz) tins whole tomatoes

60 ml (2 fl oz/¼ cup) extra virgin olive oil

6 anchovy fillets in oil

4 garlic cloves, minced

½ — ¾ teaspoon dried chilli flakes

180 g (6½ oz) pitted black olives

3 teaspoons salted baby capers, drained and rinsed

sea salt and freshly cracked black pepper

500 g (1 lb 2 oz) fresh or dried spaghetti

chopped parsley, to serve

freshly grated pecorino, to serve

Tip the tomatoes into a bowl and lightly crush them with your hands.

Heat the oil in a large frying pan over medium — low heat. Add the anchovies, garlic and chilli flakes and sauté for 2 — 3 minutes, until the anchovies begin to break down and melt into the oil. Increase the heat to medium and add the crushed tomatoes, olives and capers. Cook, stirring occasionally, for 12 — 15 minutes, until slightly thickened, then season to taste with pepper and a little salt, if necessary.

Meanwhile, bring a large saucepan of salted water to the boil and cook the pasta until al dente. Drain and add the pasta to the sauce, tossing through to combine.

Divide the puttanesca among warmed pasta bowls, top with chopped parsley and grated pecorino and serve.

PARSLEY & WALNUT PESTO
WITH FUSILLI COL BUCO

SERVES 4—6

500 g (1 lb 2 oz) dried fusilli
col buco

PARSLEY AND WALNUT PESTO

65 g (2¼ oz) toasted walnuts, plus
extra, chopped, to serve

80 g (2¾ oz) parsley leaves

2—3 garlic cloves

50 g (1¾ oz/½ cup) finely grated
fresh parmesan, plus extra shaved
parmesan, to serve

2 teaspoons lemon zest

1 tablespoon freshly squeezed
lemon juice

pinch of dried chilli flakes (optional)

125 ml (4 fl oz/½ cup) extra virgin
olive oil

sea salt and freshly cracked
black pepper

Cook the pasta in a large saucepan of salted boiling water until al dente.

Meanwhile, to make the pesto, place the walnuts, parsley, garlic, parmesan, lemon zest and juice and chilli flakes (if using) in the bowl of a food processor and pulse to combine. With the motor running, slowly drizzle in the oil and process to a chunky paste. Taste and season well with salt and pepper.

Drain the pasta, reserving 125 ml (4 fl oz/½ cup) of the pasta cooking water. Return the pasta to the pan and stir through the pesto, adding the pasta water little by little until you reach the desired consistency.

Divide the pasta among warmed pasta bowls and serve sprinkled with a few extra chopped walnuts and shavings of parmesan.

SPAGHETTI & MEATBALLS

SERVES 6 — 8

165 ml (5½ fl oz) olive oil

1 onion, finely diced

2 garlic cloves, minced

400 g (14 oz) tin fire-roasted tomatoes (or regular tinned tomatoes)

500 ml (17 fl oz/2 cups) passata (puréed tomatoes)

1 fresh or dried bay leaf

handful of basil leaves, plus extra to serve

150 g (5½ oz/1 cup) plain (all-purpose) flour

600 g (1 lb 5 oz) dried spaghetti

MEATBALLS

60 g (2 oz/¾ cup) fresh breadcrumbs

60 ml (2 fl oz/¼ cup) full-cream (whole) milk

400 g (14 oz) minced (ground) pork

400 g (14 oz) minced (ground) beef

1 small onion, finely chopped

1 free-range egg, beaten

40 g (1½ oz) freshly grated parmesan, plus extra to serve

2 garlic cloves, minced

small handful of chopped parsley

40 g (1½ oz) thinly sliced prosciutto, finely diced

1 teaspoon fine sea salt

¼ teaspoon freshly cracked black pepper

To make the meatballs, soak the breadcrumbs in the milk for 15 minutes, then drain and discard any excess milk. Place the soaked breadcrumbs in a large bowl with the remaining meatball ingredients and mix well with your hands to combine. Shape into 40 even-sized meatballs and set aside in the fridge for 20 — 30 minutes.

Heat 2 tablespoons of the oil in a large saucepan over medium heat. Sauté the onion for 5 — 7 minutes, then add the garlic and cook for a further 1 minute or until the onion is translucent.

Tip the tomatoes into a bowl and lightly crush them with your hands. Add the tomatoes, passata and bay leaf to the pan, stir well and simmer over low heat for 15 — 20 minutes. Season to taste with salt and pepper and stir through the basil leaves.

Meanwhile, place the flour in a bowl, then roll the meatballs in the flour, dusting off any excess.

Heat the remaining oil in a large frying pan over medium heat and, working in batches, add the meatballs and cook, turning frequently, until browned all over.

Add the browned meatballs to the sauce and simmer for a further 20 — 25 minutes, until the meatballs are cooked through.

While the meatballs and sauce are simmering, bring a large saucepan of salted water to the boil and cook the spaghetti until al dente. Drain.

Divide the pasta among warmed pasta bowls and ladle over the sauce and meatballs. Serve with plenty of freshly grated parmesan and a few extra basil leaves scattered over the top.

GRILLED LOBSTER TAILS WITH GARLICKY SALSA VERDE BUTTER

SERVES 4

250 g (9 oz) butter, softened

6 garlic cloves, minced

3 tablespoons chopped parsley leaves, plus extra to serve

2 tablespoons chopped basil leaves

2 tablespoons chopped tarragon leaves

2 tablespoons snipped chives

1 teaspoon chopped rosemary leaves

2 teaspoons salted baby capers, drained and rinsed

½ teaspoon dried chilli flakes

zest and juice of 1 lemon, plus extra wedges to serve

sea salt and freshly cracked black pepper, to taste

2 tablespoons extra virgin olive oil

4 x 250 g (9 oz) lobster tails, cleaned and split in half lengthways

360 g (12½ oz) fresh or dried chitarra or spaghetti

25 g (¾ oz/¼ cup) Pangrattato (see page 22)

Place the butter, garlic, herbs, capers, chilli flakes and lemon zest and juice in the bowl of a food processor and blitz until well combined. Season well with salt and pepper, then divide the salsa verde butter in half and set aside.

Preheat a barbecue grill to medium. Brush the lobster tails with a little of the olive oil and place, flesh side down, on the grill. Cook for about 4 minutes or until the shells turn bright red, then turn over and slather the lobster tails with half the salsa verde butter. Cook for a further 3 — 4 minutes or until the lobster meat is opaque and just cooked through.

Meanwhile, cook the pasta in a large saucepan of salted boiling water to 1 minute less than al dente. Drain and reserve 125 ml (4 fl oz/½ cup) of the pasta cooking water.

Melt the remaining salsa verde butter in the saucepan you used to cook the pasta over medium heat. Add a little of the pasta water and stir until the sauce starts to emulsify. Return the pasta to the pan and toss through the sauce for 1 — 2 minutes, adding a little more pasta water, if necessary, to achieve the desired consistency.

Divide the pasta among four warm serving plates and top with a buttery grilled lobster tail. Sprinkle over the pangrattato and extra parsley, and serve with lemon wedges on the side for squeezing over.

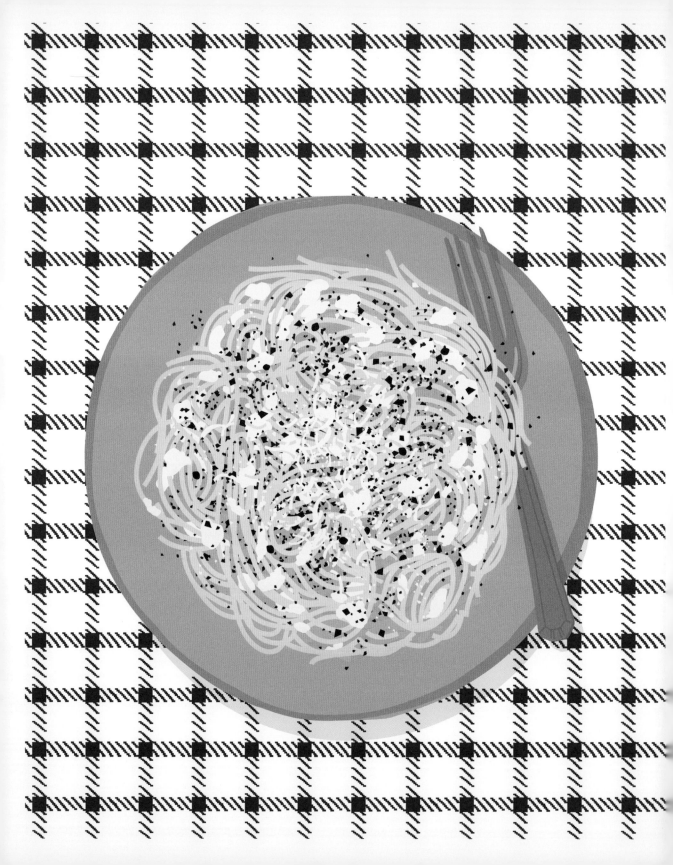

CACIO E PEPE

SERVES 4 — 6

1 tablespoon whole black peppercorns

400 g (14 oz) fresh or dried bucatini

300 g (10 oz) finely grated fresh pecorino

Lightly toast the peppercorns in a dry frying pan over medium — high heat for 40 — 50 seconds, until fragrant and beginning to pop in the pan. Transfer to a mortar and pestle and lightly crush. Set aside.

Bring a large saucepan of salted water to the boil and cook the pasta until al dente. Drain, reserving 500 ml (17 fl oz/2 cups) of the pasta cooking water.

Pour 250 ml (8½ fl oz/1 cup) of the pasta water into a large saucepan over medium — high heat and add the drained pasta. Sprinkle over one-third of the cheese and 3 teaspoons of the pepper. Use tongs to quickly and gently toss the cheese and pepper through the pasta to coat. Reduce the heat to low, add half the remaining cheese and half of the remaining water. Continue tossing until the cheese has melted and the sauce is creamy. Add more water if necessary to achieve the desired consistency.

Divide the pasta among warmed pasta bowls and top with the remaining pecorino and pepper.

CAPELLINI ALLA CHECCA

SERVES 4—6

500 g (1 lb 2 oz) dried capellini (angel hair pasta)

125 ml (4 fl oz/½ cup) extra virgin olive oil, plus extra for drizzling

30 g (1 oz) finely grated fresh parmesan, plus extra to serve

sea salt and freshly cracked black pepper

500 g (1 lb 2 oz) heirloom cherry tomatoes, halved

400 g (14 oz) baby bocconcini

½ bunch basil, leaves picked

Cook the pasta in a large saucepan of salted boiling water until al dente. Drain, reserving 60 ml (2 fl oz/¼ cup) of the pasta cooking water.

Place a saucepan over medium—low heat, add the oil and just warm through. Add the pasta to the pan, along with the cooking water and parmesan and toss to coat. Season well with salt and pepper, then remove from the heat and transfer the pasta to a large serving bowl. Toss through the tomato halves, bocconcini and basil.

Serve with plenty of extra grated parmesan and a drizzle of oil on top.

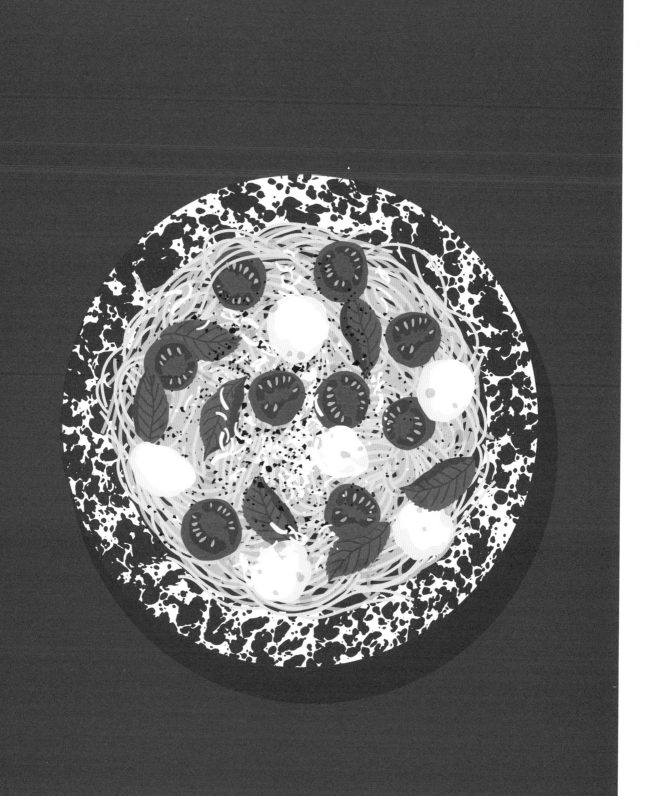

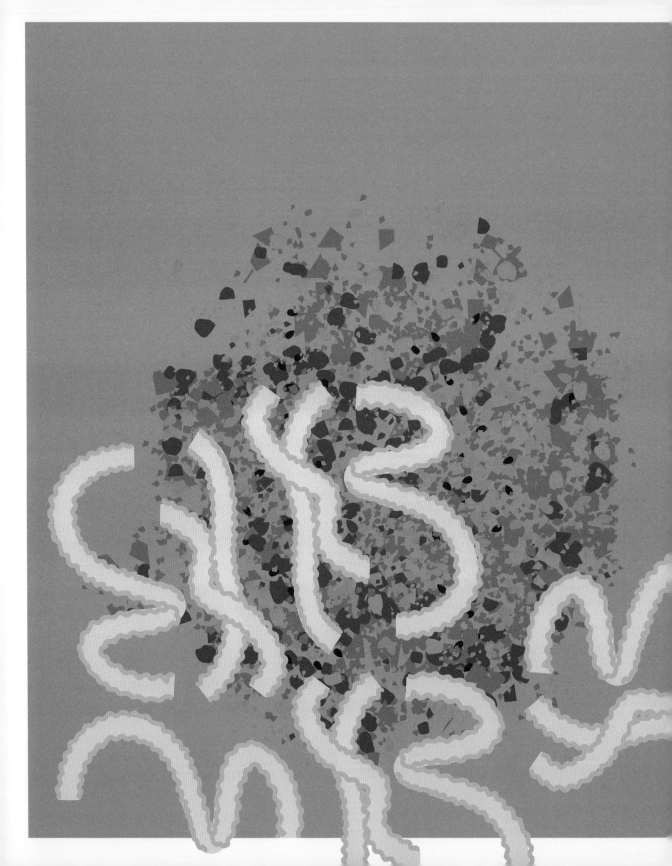

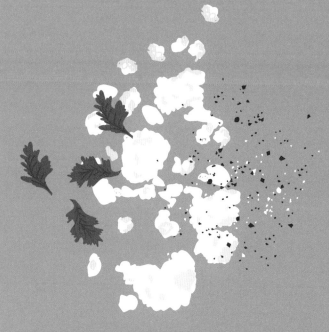

FLAT &
RIBBON PASTA

LASAGNE

SERVES AT LEAST 8

60 ml (2 fl oz/$\frac{1}{4}$ cup) olive oil

1 onion, finely diced

1 carrot, finely diced

1 celery stalk, finely diced

100 g (3$\frac{1}{2}$ oz) guanciale, diced

3 garlic cloves, minced

425 g (15 oz) minced (ground) beef

425 g (15 oz) minced (ground) pork

2 teaspoons dried basil

1 teaspoon dried oregano

$\frac{1}{4}$ teaspoon ground allspice

250 ml (8$\frac{1}{2}$ fl oz/1 cup) white wine

2 tablespoons tomato paste (concentrated purée)

2 x 400 g (14 oz) tins whole tomatoes

500 ml (17 fl oz/2 cups) passata (puréed) tomatoes

370 ml (12$\frac{1}{2}$ fl oz) chicken stock

2 fresh or dried bay leaves

sea salt and black pepper

large handful chopped basil leaves

1 kg (2 lb 3 oz) firm ricotta

50 g (1$\frac{3}{4}$ oz/$\frac{1}{2}$ cup) grated parmesan

1 free-range egg, beaten

500 g (1 lb 2 oz) dried lasagne

1 x quantity Béchamel sauce with parmesan (see page 20)

500 g (1 lb 2 oz) buffalo mozzarella

Heat the oil in a large saucepan over medium heat. Add the onion, carrot and celery and sauté for 8 — 10 minutes, until the onion is translucent and the vegetables are lightly caramelised. Add the guanciale and cook, stirring occasionally, for a further 3 — 4 minutes. Add the garlic, then crumble in the minced beef and pork, along with the dried herbs and allspice. Increase the heat to medium — high and cook, stirring frequently, for about 10 minutes, until the meat is well browned. Add the wine and deglaze the pan for 3 — 4 minutes.

Stir through the tomato paste and cook for 2 — 3 minutes. Tip the tomatoes into a bowl and lightly crush them with your hands, then add to the pan, along with the passata, stock and bay leaves. Reduce the heat to low and simmer, stirring occasionally, for 1 hour. Season to taste with salt and pepper, then stir through half the basil. Simmer for a further 30 — 40 minutes, or until reduced to a thick, rich sauce.

Combine the ricotta, half the parmesan, the egg and the remaining basil leaves in a large bowl. Set aside.

Bring a large saucepan of salted water to the boil and cook the lasagne until al dente. Drain and set aside.

Preheat the oven to 180°C (350°F).

To assemble the lasagne, spread one-third of the ragu in the bottom of a large baking dish and top with one-third of the lasagne, followed by one-third of the ricotta filling, béchamel and mozzarella. Repeat this layering, finishing with a layer mozzarella, and sprinkle the remaining parmesan over the top.

Bake in the oven for 30 — 40 minutes, until the sauce is bubbling and the top is lightly golden. Rest for 5 — 10 minutes before serving.

PAPPARDELLE WITH BEEF CHEEK RAGU

SERVES 6

900 g (2 lb) beef cheeks, diced into 7 cm (2¾ in) chunks

sea salt and freshly cracked black pepper

2 tablespoons plain (all-purpose) flour

60 ml (2 fl oz/¼ cup) extra virgin olive oil

1 large onion, finely diced

1 carrot, finely diced

1 celery stalk, finely diced

4 garlic cloves, minced

2 thyme sprigs

2 oregano sprigs

½ teaspoon rosemary leaves

500 ml (17 fl oz/2 cups) red wine

750 ml (25½ fl oz/3 cups) beef stock

3 tablespoons tomato paste (concentrated purée)

2 tablespoons chopped parsley

500 g (1 lb 2 oz) fresh or dried pappardelle

freshly grated parmesan, to serve

Preheat the oven to 170°C (340°F).

Season the beef cheeks with salt and pepper and dust with the flour.

Heat the oil in a large flameproof casserole dish over medium heat and, working in batches, sear the beef on all sides until well browned. Transfer to a plate and set aside.

Add the onion, carrot and celery to the dish and sauté for 7 — 8 minutes until softened, then add the garlic and cook for a further 1 minute. Return the beef to the dish and add the herbs and wine. Increase the heat to medium — high and bring to the boil, then reduce the heat to low and simmer for 10 — 12 minutes. Add the stock and tomato paste, stir to combine, then cover and place in the oven for 2½ — 3 hours, until the meat is fork-tender and falling apart.

Remove the dish from the oven and use two forks to shred the beef. Season to taste with salt and pepper, then stir through the parsley.

Cook the pappardelle in a large saucepan of salted boiling water until al dente. Drain and add to the pasta sauce, tossing to combine.

Divide the pasta among warm pasta bowls and serve with parmesan on the side.

LINGUINE VONGOLE

SERVES 4—6

500 g (1 lb 2 oz) fresh or dried linguini

60 ml (2 fl oz/¼ cup) extra virgin olive oil, plus extra for drizzling

60 g (2 oz) butter

4 garlic cloves, minced

1 — 2 red bird's eye chillies, thinly sliced

1 kg (2 lb 3 oz) clams, purged (see Note)

125 ml (4 fl oz/½ cup) white wine

large handful of parsley, chopped

zest and juice of 1 large lemon, plus extra lemon wedges to serve

sea salt and freshly cracked black pepper

Cook the linguini in a large saucepan of salted boiling water until al dente. Drain, reserving 125 ml (4 fl oz/½ cup) of the pasta cooking water.

Meanwhile, heat the oil and butter in a large frying pan over medium heat. Add the garlic and chilli and sauté for 1 — 2 minutes, until fragrant but not coloured. Increase the heat to medium — high, add the clams, wine and half the parsley, then cover and cook for 4 minutes or until the clams open. (Discard any that do not open.)

Reduce the heat to medium, add the linguini, lemon zest and juice and quickly toss everything together. Season to taste with salt and pepper, adding some of the reserved pasta water to loosen the mixture, if necessary.

Divide the linguine among warm pasta bowls and sprinkle over the remaining parsley. Drizzle over a little extra oil and serve with lemon wedges on the side.

NOTE:

Clams bought from the supermarket usually come already cleaned and purged, but if you are lucky enough to buy them from a small supplier, local fisherman or you've dug them up yourself, you will need to prepare them before cooking. Give the clams a good rinse under cold running water, then transfer to a colander that fits inside a large saucepan and cover the clams with cold salted water. (A good ratio for salted water is 35 g/1¼ oz sea salt to 1 litre/34 fl oz/4 cups water. Alternatively, use fresh seawater if you live by the sea.) Soak the clams for 40 — 60 minutes (this encourages them to spit out, or purge, any sandy grit). Remove the clams from the water, rinse again and use as directed.

FETTUCCINE ALFREDO

SERVES 4 — 6

500 g (1 lb 2 oz) fresh or dried fettuccine

250 g (9 oz) butter, diced

250 g (9 oz) parmesan, finely grated, plus extra to serve

sea salt and freshly cracked black pepper

Cook the pasta in a large saucepan of salted boiling water to 1 minute less than al dente. Reserve 500 ml (17 fl oz/2 cups) of the pasta cooking water, then drain the pasta and set aside.

Heat 400 ml (14 fl oz) of the pasta cooking water in a large saucepan over medium heat. Bring the liquid to a simmer and gradually add the butter, whisking to incorporate. Sprinkle in the cheese a little at a time, whisking to blend and create a sauce.

Reduce the heat slightly and add the pasta. Use tongs to gently, but quickly, mix everything together, ensuring that the pasta is well-coated in the cheesy, buttery sauce. Add the remaining pasta water, if necessary, to achieve a silky texture. Season well with salt and pepper.

Serve in warm pasta bowls with extra parmesan on the side for sprinkling over the top.

TAGLIATELLE BOLOGNAISE

SERVES 4 — 6

2 tablespoons extra virgin olive oil

40 g (1½ oz) butter

1 carrot, finely diced

1 large onion, finely diced

1 celery stalk, finely diced

100 g (3½ oz) pancetta, diced

3 garlic cloves, minced

300 g (10½ oz) minced (ground) veal

350 g (12½ oz) minced (ground) pork

¼ teaspoon ground allspice

pinch of ground cloves

250 ml (8½ fl oz/1 cup) red wine

3 tablespoons tomato paste
(concentrated purée)

750 g (25½ oz) whole
tinned tomatoes

250 ml (8½ fl oz/1 cup) chicken stock

1 fresh or dried bay leaf

250 ml (8½ fl oz/1 cup) full-cream
(whole) milk

sea salt and freshly cracked
black pepper

500 g (1 lb 2 oz) fresh or dried
tagliatelle

freshly grated parmesan, to serve

Heat the oil and butter in a large frying pan over medium heat. Add the carrot, onion and celery and sauté for 8 — 10 minutes, until the onion is translucent and the vegetables are lightly caramelised. Add the pancetta and cook, stirring occasionally, for a further 3 — 4 minutes. Add the garlic, then crumble in the minced veal and pork, along with the allspice and cloves. Increase the heat to medium — high and cook, stirring frequently, for about 10 minutes, until the meat is well browned. Add the wine and deglaze the pan for 3 — 4 minutes, then stir through the tomato paste and cook for 2 — 3 minutes.

Tip the tomatoes into a bowl and lightly crush them with your hands, then add to the pan along with the stock and bay leaf. Reduce the heat to low and simmer, stirring occasionally, for 1 hour. Add the milk, season to taste with salt and pepper and cook for a further 20 — 30 minutes, until reduced to a thick, rich sauce.

Cook the tagliatelle in a large saucepan of salted boiling water until al dente. Drain and toss the pasta through the sauce.

Serve the tagliatelle bolognaise in warm pasta bowls with grated parmesan on the side for sprinkling over.

BEETROOT TAGLIATELLE WITH SAUTÉED BEETROOT LEAVES, TOASTED WALNUTS & GOAT'S CHEESE

SERVES 4 — 6

60 ml (2 fl oz/¼ cup) extra virgin olive oil, plus extra for drizzling

60 g (2 oz) butter

100 g (3½ oz) French shallots, thinly sliced

4 garlic cloves, thinly sliced

1½ teaspoons lemon thyme leaves

1 teaspoon rosemary leaves, finely chopped

zest of 1 lemon

500 g (1 lb 2 oz) baby beetroot (beet) leaves

1 x quantity Beetroot pasta dough (see page 14), cut into tagliatelle

200 g (7 oz) ashed goat's cheese, crumbled

100 g (3½ oz/1 cup) walnut halves, toasted

sea salt and freshly cracked black pepper

Heat the oil and butter in a large frying pan over medium — low heat. Add the shallot, garlic, herbs and lemon zest and sauté for about 3 minutes, until the shallot is soft. Add the beetroot leaves and toss through for 1 — 2 minutes, until wilted.

Meanwhile, bring a large saucepan of salted water to the boil and cook the tagliatelle until al dente. Drain, reserving 125 ml (4 fl oz/½ cup) of the pasta cooking water, then add the tagliatelle to the beetroot leaf mixture, along with the goat's cheese and walnuts. Toss everything together and season to taste with salt and pepper. Add a little pasta water to loosen the sauce, if desired.

Divide the tagliatelle among warm pasta bowls and serve with an extra drizzle of extra virgin olive oil.

SQUID INK LINGUINE WITH CRAB & SEA URCHIN ROE

SERVES 4—6

1 x quantity Squid ink pasta (see page 14), cut into linguine or use 500 g (1 lb 2 oz) dried squid ink linguine

80 ml (2½ fl oz/⅓ cup) extra virgin olive oil, plus extra for drizzling

80 g (2¾ oz) butter

1 large French shallot, finely diced

4 garlic cloves, minced

½ teaspoon dried chilli flakes, or to taste

zest and juice of 1 large lemon

185 ml (6 fl oz/¾ cup) white wine

500 g (1 lb 2 oz) fresh lump crab meat

small handful of parsley, chopped

sea salt and freshly cracked black pepper

16—24 sea urchin roe (see Note)

Bring a large saucepan of salted water to the boil and cook the pasta to 1 minute less than al dente. Drain, reserving 125 ml (4 fl oz/½ cup) of the pasta cooking water.

Meanwhile, heat the oil and butter in a large frying pan over medium—low heat. Add the shallot and garlic and sauté for 3—4 minutes until translucent, soft and fragrant. Add the chilli flakes, lemon zest and juice and white wine, then increase the heat and simmer rapidly for 3—4 minutes. Toss through the crab, parsley and pasta, and season to taste with salt and pepper. Add a little pasta water and continue to toss for a further 1—2 minutes to emulsify the sauce.

Divide the linguine among warm pasta bowls, top with the sea urchin roe and serve with a good drizzle of oil.

NOTE:

Sea urchin roe can be purchased from fish markets and some fishmongers.

CREAMY PUMPKIN FETTUCINE

SERVES 4—6

1 kg (2 lb 3 oz) butternut pumpkin (squash), peeled, deseeded and cut into 4 cm (1½ in) chunks

1 onion, cut into 4 cm (1½ in) chunks

6 garlic cloves, smashed

80 ml (2½ fl oz/⅓ cup) extra virgin olive oil

sea salt and freshly cracked black pepper

3 tablespoons olive oil

20—24 sage leaves

500 g (1 lb 2 oz) fresh or dried fettuccine

375 ml (12½ fl oz/1½ cups) chicken or vegetable stock

200 g (7 oz) crème fraîche

½ teaspoon freshly grated nutmeg

2 tablespoons toasted pine nuts

freshly grated parmesan, to serve

Preheat the oven to 200°C (400°F). Line a baking tray with baking paper.

Toss the pumpkin, onion, garlic and extra virgin olive oil in a bowl and season with salt and pepper. Transfer to the prepared tray and roast for 20—25 minutes, until the pumpkin is soft and cooked through.

Meanwhile, heat the olive oil in a frying pan over medium—high heat. Add the sage leaves and fry (be careful as they can spit) for 2—3 minutes, until crisp. Drain on paper towel and set aside.

Bring a large saucepan of salted water to the boil and cook the fettuccine until al dente. Drain, reserving 125 ml (4 fl oz/½ cup) of the pasta cooking water.

While the pasta is cooking, place the pumpkin mixture, stock, crème fraîche and nutmeg in a blender and purée. Taste and season with a little more salt and pepper, if necessary, and transfer to a large bowl.

Toss the just-drained fettuccine through the warm pumpkin sauce, adding the reserved pasta water as needed to achieve a creamy, lush sauce. Twirl the pasta into warm pasta bowls, top with the reserved fried sage leaves, pine nuts and parmesan, and serve straight away.

HOT SMOKED SALMON, CRÈME FRAÎCHE & PEAS WITH MAFALDINE

SERVES 4—6

400 g (14 oz) fresh or dried mafaldine (see Note)

80 g (2¾ oz) butter

1½ tablespoons extra virgin olive oil

2 garlic cloves, minced

2 — 3 lemon thyme sprigs, leaves picked

2 teaspoons salted baby capers, drained, rinsed and chopped

zest of 3 lemons

juice of 2 lemons, plus extra wedges to serve

350 g (12½ oz) crème fraîche

350 g (12½ oz) hot smoked salmon, flaked

195 g (7 oz/1¼ cups) frozen peas, thawed

freshly cracked black pepper

mint leaves, to serve

Cook the pasta in a large saucepan of salted boiling water until al dente. Drain, reserving 250 ml (8½ fl oz/1 cup) of the pasta cooking water.

Meanwhile, heat the butter and oil in a large frying pan over medium heat. Add the garlic, thyme leaves, capers and two-thirds of the lemon zest and cook for 1 — 1½ minutes until fragrant and the garlic has softened.

Add the pasta to the pan, along with 60 ml (2 fl oz/¼ cup) of the pasta water and the lemon juice. Toss the mixture together for 1 — 2 minutes, then stir through the crème fraîche. Toss the flaked salmon and peas through the pasta to warm and season well with black pepper. Add a little more pasta water to thin the sauce if desired.

Divide the pasta among warm pasta bowls and scatter the remaining lemon zest and a few mint leaves over the top. Serve with lemon wedges on the side for squeezing over.

NOTE:

Mafaldine pasta is a type of ribbon pasta. It can be purchased from Italian delis and specialist stores.

LEMON TAGLIATELLE WITH ASPARAGUS, ROCKET & RICOTTA

SERVES 4 — 6

500 g (1 lb 2 oz) asparagus, woody ends removed, spears quartered

2 tablespoons extra virgin olive oil, plus extra for drizzling

40 g (1½ oz) butter

1 French shallot, finely diced

zest and juice of 2 lemons

1 x quantity Lemon pasta, cut into tagliatelle (see page 14)

375 g (13 oz/1½ cups) good-quality sheep's milk ricotta

50 g (1¾ oz/½ cup) finely grated fresh pecorino

50 g (1¾ oz) wild rocket (arugula)

2 tablespoons finely chopped dill

2 tablespoons finely snipped chives

sea salt and freshly cracked black pepper

40 g (1½ oz/¼ cup) smoked almonds, chopped

Bring a large saucepan of salted water to the boil over high heat and blanch the asparagus for about 1 minute, until just tender. Using tongs, remove the asparagus and refresh in iced water. Set aside.

Heat the oil and butter in a large frying pan over medium — low heat. Add the shallot and sauté for 3 — 4 minutes until soft and translucent. Add the lemon zest and juice and cook for a further 1 minute.

Meanwhile, bring the water in the pan back to the boil, add the tagliatelle and cook until al dente. Drain, reserving 125 ml (4 fl oz/½ cup) of the pasta cooking water, then add the tagliatelle to the shallot mixture along with the asparagus, ricotta, pecorino, rocket and herbs. Toss through a little of the pasta water to melt the cheese, and season to taste with salt and pepper. Toss again, adding more pasta water, if necessary, to create a creamy sauce that clings to the pasta.

Divide the tagliatelle among warm pasta bowls, scatter over the chopped almonds and serve drizzled with a little extra oil.

SHORT-CUT PASTA

PASTA E FAGIOLI

SERVES 4—6

2 tablespoons extra virgin olive oil

1 small onion, finely diced

1 carrot, finely diced

1 celery stalk, finely diced

2 garlic cloves, minced

1 teaspoon finely chopped rosemary leaves

400 g (14 oz) tin crushed tomatoes

1.5 litres (51 fl oz/6 cups) chicken stock

1 small smoked ham hock

1 fresh or dried bay leaf

400 g (14 oz) tin cannellini beans, drained and rinsed

small handful of parsley leaves, chopped

100 g (3½ oz) dried elbow macaroni or ditalini pasta

sea salt and freshly cracked black pepper

freshly grated parmesan, to serve

Heat the oil in a large saucepan over medium heat. Add the onion, carrot and celery and sauté for 5—7 minutes, until the onion becomes translucent and the vegetables are soft. Add the garlic and rosemary and sauté for 1 minute or until fragrant. Add the tomatoes, stock, ham hock and bay leaf and bring to the boil. Reduce the heat to medium—low and simmer for 50—60 minutes, until the ham hock is cooked through.

Remove the ham hock from the soup and set aside to cool. Remove the meat from the bone and shred into bite-sized pieces. Discard the skin and bone and return the ham to the soup. Add the beans and parsley and stir to combine.

Cook the pasta in a large saucepan of salted boiling water until al dente. Drain and set aside.

Transfer 500 ml (17 fl oz/2 cups) of the ham soup to a blender and purée until smooth. Return the mixture to the pan, add the pasta and stir through. Season to taste with salt, if needed, and pepper.

Divide the pasta soup among warm pasta bowls and serve topped with grated parmesan.

GEMELLI WITH AVOCADO, BASIL & LEMON SAUCE

SERVES 4—6

500 g (1 lb 2 oz) dried gemelli

2 large avocados, peeled and stone removed

zest and juice of 1 lemon

2 garlic cloves, peeled

1 tablespoon nutritional yeast flakes

1½ tablespoons extra virgin olive oil

large handful of basil leaves, plus extra to serve

sea salt and freshly cracked black pepper

Vegan parmesan (see page 21), to serve

Cook the gemelli in a large saucepan of salted boiling water, until al dente. Drain, reserving 125 ml (4 fl oz/½ cup) of the pasta cooking water.

Meanwhile, place the avocado, lemon zest and juice, garlic, nutritional yeast flakes and basil leaves in a blender and blitz until smooth and silky. Season to taste with salt and pepper and transfer to a large bowl.

Toss the gemelli through the sauce, adding a little of the reserved pasta water to thin the sauce, if desired. Check the seasoning and adjust if necessary.

Divide the pasta among warm pasta bowls, scatter over a few extra basil leaves and serve with vegan parmesan on the side.

LAMB RAGU WITH RIGATONI

SERVES 4—6

900 g (2 lb) boneless lamb shoulder, cut into 5 cm (2 in) cubes

sea salt and freshly cracked black pepper

60 ml (2 fl oz/¼ cup) extra virgin olive oil

1 carrot, diced

2 onions, diced

4 garlic cloves, thinly sliced

500 ml (17 fl oz/2 cups) red wine

900 g (2 lb) tinned whole tomatoes

1 rosemary sprig, leaves picked

2 sage sprigs, leaves picked

155 g (5½ oz/1 cup) frozen peas

500 g (1 lb 2 oz) dried rigatoni

freshly grated parmesan, to serve

Preheat the oven to 160°C (320°F). Season the lamb well with salt and pepper. Heat the oil in a large flameproof casserole dish over medium—high heat and, working in batches, sear the lamb on all sides for 6—7 minutes, until evenly browned. Transfer to a plate and set aside.

Reduce the heat slightly, add the carrot and onion and sauté for 8—9 minutes, until softened and beginning to caramelise. Add the garlic and cook for 1 minute or until just fragrant, then add the wine and cook, stirring, until reduced by half.

Tip the tomatoes into a bowl and lightly crush them with your hands, then add to the pan along with the herbs. Return the lamb to the dish along with any juices and stir through.

Cover the dish, transfer to the oven and cook for about 2½ hours, until the ragu has reduced to a thick, rich sauce and the lamb is fork-tender. Stir through the peas and season to taste with salt and pepper.

While the sauce is cooking, bring a large saucepan of salted water to the boil. Add the rigatoni and cook until al dente. Drain and set aside.

Shred any larger chunks of lamb into bite-sized pieces. Add the rigatoni to the ragu and stir through to completely coat the pasta.

Divide the ragu among warm pasta bowls and serve with grated parmesan.

PENNE ARRABIATA

SERVES 4 — 6

500 g (1 lb 2 oz) fresh or dried penne

3 tablespoons extra virgin olive oil

4 garlic cloves, minced

1 teaspoon dried chilli flakes

2 x 400 g (14 oz) tins whole tomatoes

sea salt and freshly cracked black pepper

handful of basil leaves

70 g (2½ oz) finely grated fresh pecorino

Cook the penne in a large saucepan of salted boiling water to 1 minute less than al dente. Drain, reserving 125 ml (4 fl oz/½ cup) of the pasta cooking water.

Meanwhile, heat the oil in a large saucepan over medium heat. Add the garlic and chilli flakes and sauté for 1 minute or until fragrant.

Tip the tomatoes into a bowl and lightly crush them with your hands, then add to the pan and cook, stirring occasionally, for 10 — 15 minutes, until slightly reduced and thickened. Season to taste with salt and pepper.

Add the penne to the pan, along with 60 ml (2 fl oz/¼ cup) of the pasta water. Stir and cook for a further 1 — 2 minutes, until the pasta is al dente, then add the basil leaves and half the pecorino and toss to combine. Add a little more pasta water to slightly thin the sauce, if desired.

Divide the pasta among warm pasta bowls and serve with the remaining pecorino sprinkled over the top.

MAC 'N' CHEESE

SERVES 6

140 g (5 oz) butter

500 g (1 lb 2 oz) dried elbow macaroni

35 g (1¼ oz/¼ cup) plain (all-purpose) flour

½ teaspoon ground white pepper

½ teaspoon mustard powder

½ teaspoon garlic powder

½ teaspoon onion powder

¼ teaspoon freshly grated nutmeg

good pinch of cayenne pepper

500 ml (17 fl oz/2 cups) full-cream (whole) milk

250 ml (8½ fl oz/1 cup) pure cream

1 teaspoon fine sea salt

400 g (14 oz) sharp cheddar, grated

100 g (3½ oz/¾ cup) grated gruyère

50 g (1¾ oz/½ cup) finely grated fresh parmesan

25 g (1 oz/½ cup) panko breadcrumbs

sea salt and freshly cracked black pepper

Preheat the oven to 180°C (350°F). Grease a 33 cm x 23 cm (13¼ in x 9 in) baking dish with 20 g (¾ oz) of the butter and set aside.

Cook the macaroni in a large saucepan of salted boiling water to 1 minute less than al dente. Drain and set aside.

Melt 60 g (2 oz) of the remaining butter in a large saucepan over medium—low heat. Whisk in the flour and spices and cook, whisking constantly, for 2 minutes or until a roux forms and the mixture resembles wet sand. Gradually whisk in the milk, a little at a time, followed by the cream, until you have a rich, creamy, lump-free sauce. Add the salt, increase the heat to medium and simmer for 4—5 minutes, until thickened.

Remove the sauce from the heat and whisk in the cheddar and gruyère, a handful at a time, until well incorporated. When all the cheese has melted, add the macaroni and stir to completely coat the pasta.

Pour the mixture into the greased baking dish, sprinkle over the parmesan and breadcrumbs and lightly season with salt and pepper. Dot the remaining butter over the top, then transfer to the oven and bake for 15 minutes or until bubbling.

Preheat the grill (broiler) to medium—high. Pop the mac 'n' cheese under the grill for 2—3 minutes to crisp and brown the parmesan and breadcrumbs.

Serve immediately.

VEGAN MAC 'N' CHEESE

SERVES 4—6

500 g (1 lb 2 oz) dried conchiglie

235 g (8½ oz/1½ cups) raw cashews, soaked in cold water for 6—8 hours or overnight, drained

250 ml (8½ fl oz/1 cup) vegetable stock, heated

25 g (1 oz/½ cup) nutritional yeast flakes

50 ml (1¾ fl oz) freshly squeezed lemon juice

2 tablespoons white miso paste

1 tablespoon extra virgin olive oil

2 teaspoons dijon mustard

1 teaspoon onion powder

½ teaspoon garlic powder

¼ teaspoon smoked paprika

¼ teaspoon ground turmeric

sea salt and freshly cracked black pepper

handful of parsley leaves, chopped, to serve

Vegan pangrattato (see page 22), to serve

Vegan parmesan (see page 21) or finely grated macadamia nuts, to serve

Cook the pasta in a large saucepan of salted boiling water until al dente. Drain, reserving 125 ml (4 fl oz/½ cup) of the pasta cooking water.

Meanwhile, place the cashews, stock, nutritional yeast flakes, lemon juice, miso, oil, mustard and spices in a blender or the small bowl of a food processor and blend until silky smooth (see Note). Season to taste with salt and pepper and transfer to a large bowl.

Toss the drained pasta through the sauce, adding a little of the pasta water to thin the sauce, if desired. Divide the pasta among warm pasta bowls, top with the parsley, pangrattato and vegan parmesan and serve.

NOTE:

If you would like your mac 'n' cheese to have a smoky flavour, add 3 tablespoons of chipotle adobo sauce to the blender with the other ingredients.

ORECCHIETTE WITH BROCCOLI SAUCE

SERVES 4—6

600 g (1 lb 5 oz) broccoli florets, roughly chopped

500 g (1 lb 2 oz) fresh or dried orecchiette

80 ml (2½ fl oz/⅓ cup) extra virgin olive oil, plus extra for drizzling

¾ teaspoon dried chilli flakes, crushed

5—6 garlic cloves, minced

50 g (1¾ oz) tin good-quality anchovy fillets in oil

250 ml (8½ fl oz/1 cup) chicken or vegetable stock

80 g (2¾ oz) freshly grated parmesan, plus extra to serve

zest and juice of 1 lemon

sea salt and freshly cracked black pepper

1 x quantity Pangrattato (see page 22)

Set a steamer over a saucepan of boiling water and steam the broccoli until very tender. Set aside.

Cook the orecchiette in a large saucepan of salted boiling water to 1 minute less than al dente. Drain, reserving 250 ml (8½ fl oz/1 cup) of the pasta cooking water and set aside.

Meanwhile, place a large frying pan over medium — low heat and add the oil, chilli flakes, garlic and anchovies. Sauté for 3 minutes or until the anchovies begin to melt and the garlic is fragrant and golden. Add the broccoli and stock to the pan and simmer, breaking down the broccoli with the back of a wooden spoon, for 6—8 minutes, until the broccoli creates a sauce. Continue to cook, stirring occasionally, for another 6—8 minutes, until the sauce has reduced and thickened slightly. Add the orecchiette and a little of the pasta water to the pan and toss for 1—2 minutes to coat the pasta in the sauce. Sprinkle over the parmesan and stir through the lemon zest and juice. Season to taste with salt and pepper and add a little more pasta water to loosen the sauce further, if desired.

Divide the orecchiette among warm pasta bowls and top with a sprinkling of pangrattato and extra parmesan and a good drizzle of olive oil.

TROFIE PESTO ALLA GENOVESE

SERVES 4 — 6

500 g (1 lb 2 oz) fresh or dried trofie

400 g (14 oz) small new potatoes, sliced into 1 cm (½ in) thick rounds

120 g (4½ oz) green beans, trimmed and halved

PESTO ALLA GENOVESE

2 bunches of basil, leaves picked

2 — 3 garlic cloves, peeled

50 g (1¾ oz/⅓ cup) pine nuts, toasted

30 g (1 oz) finely grated fresh parmesan

125 ml (4 fl oz/½ cup) extra virgin olive oil

sea salt and freshly cracked black pepper

zest of 1 lemon (optional), plus extra to serve

1 tablespoon freshly squeezed lemon juice (optional)

To make the pesto, place the basil, garlic, pine nuts, parmesan and oil in the bowl of a food processor and blitz to a paste. Season to taste with salt, pepper and the lemon zest and juice (if using).

Cook the trofie in a large saucepan of salted boiling water until al dente. Drain, reserving 125 ml (4 fl oz/½ cup) of the pasta cooking water. Place the trofie in a large serving bowl.

Meanwhile, place the potato in a large saucepan and cover with cold water. Season well with salt, bring to the boil and cook for 6 — 8 minutes, until tender. Add the green beans in the last 3 minutes of cooking, then drain and add the potato and beans to the pasta.

Stir the pesto through the pasta mixture, adding a little of the reserved pasta water to loosen the pesto, if necessary.

Sprinkle a little lemon zest over the top and serve.

FREGOLA WITH MUSSELS

SERVES 4—6

200 g (7 oz/1 cup) dried fregola

80 ml (2½ fl oz/⅓ cup) olive oil

1 onion, diced

1 baby fennel, diced, fronds reserved

½ teaspoon dried chilli flakes, crushed

5—6 garlic cloves, minced

500 g (1 lb 2 oz) ripe cherry tomatoes

good pinch of saffron

sea salt and freshly cracked black pepper

250 ml (8½ fl oz/1 cup) white wine

250 ml (8½ fl oz/1 cup) fish stock

1 kg (2 lb 3 oz) mussels, cleaned and debearded

small handful of parsley leaves, chopped

sliced long red chilli, to serve

extra virgin olive oil, for drizzling

lemon wedges, to serve

Cook the fregola in a large saucepan of salted boiling water until al dente. Drain and set aside.

While the pasta is cooking, heat the oil in a large saucepan over medium heat. Add the onion, fennel and chilli flakes and sauté for 5—6 minutes. Stir in the garlic and cook for 1 minute, then add the cherry tomatoes and sauté for a further 6—7 minutes, until they begin to soften. Stir through the saffron and season with just a pinch of salt and lots of pepper.

Add the wine, stock and mussels to the pan, increase the heat to high and cover with a tight-fitting lid. Cook, occasionally shaking the pan, for 6—8 minutes, until the mussels have opened. (Discard any mussels that do not open.) Add the fregola and stir through the parsley.

Divide the mussels and fregola among warm pasta bowls and spoon over the sauce. Top with the reserved fennel fronds, a few slices of chilli and a drizzle of extra virgin olive oil. Serve with lemon wedges on the side for squeezing over.

FARFALLE WITH ZUCCHINI BLOSSOMS

SERVES 4

400 g (14 oz) fresh or dried farfalle

500 g (1 lb 2 oz) baby zucchini (courgettes) with blossoms attached

1 tablespoon extra virgin olive oil

40 g (1½ oz) butter

sea salt and freshly cracked black pepper

2 large garlic cloves, minced

250 g (9 oz) goat's curd

40 g (1½ oz) freshly grated pecorino, plus extra to serve

zest and juice of 1 large lemon

2 tablespoons thinly snipped garlic chives

2 tablespoons slivered pistachios, toasted

basil leaves, to serve

Cook the farfalle in a large saucepan of salted boiling water until al dente. Drain, reserving 125 ml (4 fl oz/½ cup) of the pasta cooking water.

While the pasta is cooking, remove the blossoms from the zucchini, then slice the zucchini into thin rounds. Remove and discard the stamens from the blossoms, then tear the blossoms into strips.

Heat the oil and butter in a large frying pan over medium heat. Add the sliced zucchini, season with salt and pepper and sauté for 2 minutes. Add the garlic and sauté for 1 minute or until fragrant and the zucchini is lightly golden. Toss through the zucchini blossom and cook for about 1 minute or until wilted. Remove the pan from the heat and set aside.

Place the goat's curd, pecorino, lemon zest and juice and garlic chives in a large serving bowl. Mix well and add 1 tablespoon of the pasta water to loosen the mixture. Add the farfalle and zucchini mixture and toss well to coat the pasta in the melting goat's curd sauce, adding a little more pasta water, if desired. Stir through the pistachios and top with plenty of extra grated pecorino, a few basil leaves and some more pepper, if desired. Serve immediately.

PENNE ALLA NORMA

SERVES 4—6

650 g (1 lb 7 oz) eggplants (aubergines), cut into 3 cm (1¼ in) cubes

200 ml (7 fl oz) olive oil

2 x 400 g (14 oz) tins whole tomatoes

60 ml (2 fl oz/¼ cup) extra virgin olive oil

3 garlic cloves, minced

good pinch of dried chilli flakes (optional)

sea salt and freshly cracked black pepper

500 g (1 lb 2 oz) fresh or dried penne

20 g (¾ oz) basil leaves, roughly chopped

250 g (9 oz/1 cup) good-quality sheep's milk ricotta or grated ricotta salata, to serve

Preheat the oven to 230°C (445°F). Line two baking trays with baking paper.

Toss the eggplant and olive oil together in a large bowl, then transfer to the prepared trays. Roast the eggplant for 10 minutes, then remove from the oven and give the trays a shake to turn the eggplant over. Continue to roast for a further 10 minutes or until the eggplant is golden brown and cooked through. Set aside.

Meanwhile, tip the tomatoes into a bowl and lightly crush them with your hands.

Heat the extra virgin olive oil in a large frying pan over low heat and add the garlic and chilli flakes (if using). Gently sauté for 1 minute or until fragrant, then add the crushed tomatoes and simmer, stirring occasionally, for 10—15 minutes, until slightly reduced. Season to taste with salt and pepper.

Cook the penne in a large saucepan of salted boiling water until al dente. Drain, reserving 125 ml (4 fl oz/½ cup) of the pasta cooking water.

Add the basil and penne to the pasta sauce and stir well to combine. Add a little of the reserved pasta water if you prefer a slightly thinner sauce, then stir through the roasted eggplant.

Divide the pasta among warm pasta bowls and top with dollops of sheep's milk ricotta or grated ricotta salata.

'NDUJA & TOMATO RIGATONI

SERVES 4—6

1 tablespoon extra virgin olive oil

1 onion, finely diced

120 g (4½ oz) 'nduja, casing removed
(see Note)

2—3 garlic cloves, minced

4 basil sprigs, leaves and stalks
separated

2 x 400 g (14 oz) tins whole
tomatoes

125 ml (4 fl oz/½ cup) white wine

sea salt and freshly cracked
black pepper

500 g (1 lb 2 oz) dried rigatoni

180 g (6½ oz) ball buffalo burrata

Heat the oil in a large frying pan over medium heat. Add the
onion and sauté for 5—7 minutes, until translucent. Add the
'nduja, breaking it up with the back of a wooden spoon, and
cook for 1—2 minutes, then stir in the garlic and basil stalks
and cook until fragrant. Add the tomatoes and wine, reduce the
heat to medium—low and cook for 10—12 minutes, until the
tomatoes have broken down and the sauce has thickened slightly.
Remove and discard the basil stalks and season to taste with salt
and pepper.

Meanwhile, bring a large saucepan of salted water to the boil
and cook the rigatoni until al dente. Drain and add to the pasta
sauce, stirring well to completely coat the rigatoni.

To serve, divide the rigatoni and sauce among warm pasta
bowls. Evenly tear the burrata over the top and finish with the
basil leaves.

NOTE:

*'Nduja is a soft, spreadable spicy pork sausage from Calabria. It can be
purchased from European delis and specialty butchers.*

PESTO ALLA TRAPANESE

SERVES 4 — 6

500 g (1 lb 2 oz) fresh or dried busiate

shaved ricotta salata, to serve

SICILIAN PESTO

400 g (14 oz) ripe cherry tomatoes

3 garlic cloves, peeled

handful of basil leaves

100 g (3½ oz) blanched almonds, lightly toasted

100 g (3½ oz) freshly grated pecorino

good pinch of dried chilli flakes

125 ml (4 fl oz/½ cup) extra virgin olive oil

sea salt and freshly cracked black pepper

To make the pesto, place the tomatoes, garlic, basil, almonds, pecorino and chilli flakes in the bowl of a food processor and blitz to a paste. With the motor running, slowly drizzle in the oil until completely incorporated. Transfer to a large bowl and season to taste with salt and pepper.

Cook the busiate in a large saucepan of salted boiling water until al dente. Drain and toss through the pesto until the pasta is completely coated in the sauce.

Divide the pasta among warmed pasta bowls and top with shavings of ricotta salata.

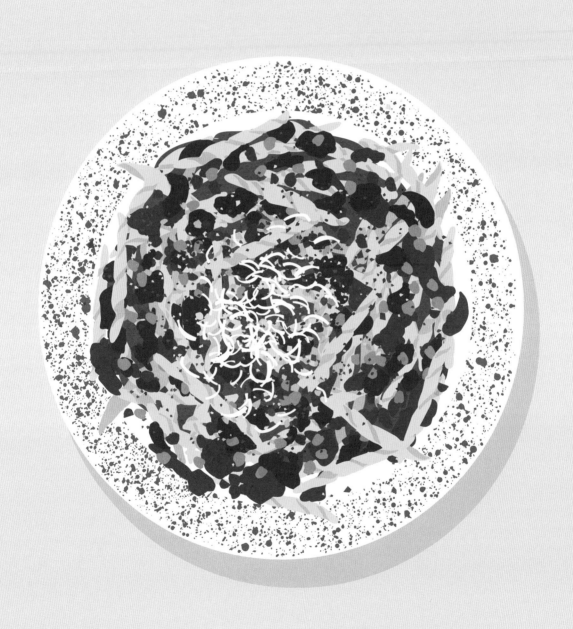

ORZO WITH PRAWNS, FETA, PARSLEY & LEMON

SERVES 4—6

60 ml (2 fl oz/¼ cup) extra virgin olive oil

40 g (1½ oz) butter

1 onion, finely diced

4 garlic cloves, minced

400 g (14 oz) dried orzo

1 litre (34 fl oz/4 cups) fish, vegetable or chicken stock

zest and juice of 1 lemon, plus extra zest and lemon wedges to serve

80 g (2¾ oz/½ cup) pitted kalamata olives

2 teaspoons salted baby capers, drained and rinsed

24 wild-caught green prawns (shrimp), peeled and deveined

200 g (7 oz) marinated artichokes, quartered

sea salt and freshly cracked black pepper

small handful of parsley, chopped

125 g (4 oz) feta, crumbled

Heat the oil and butter in a large frying pan over medium heat. Add the onion and sauté for 5—7 minutes, until soft and translucent, then add the garlic and sauté for 1 minute or until fragrant. Add the orzo and stir well to coat in the onion mixture. Cook for about 4 minutes, then add the stock, lemon zest and juice, olives and capers. Continue to cook, stirring occasionally, for a further 5—6 minutes, until the orzo is almost al dente.

Toss the prawns through the orzo and cook for 4—5 minutes, until opaque and just cooked through. Stir in the artichoke quarters and season to taste with salt and pepper. Stir through the parsley.

Divide the pasta among warmed pasta bowls and scatter over the crumbled feta and extra lemon zest. Serve with lemon wedges on the side for squeezing over.

BAKED ZITI WITH SPICY FENNEL
& PORK SAUSAGE

SERVES 8+

2 tablespoons extra virgin olive oil, plus extra for greasing

20 g (¾ oz) butter

½ onion, finely diced

650 g (1 lb 7 oz) Italian pork sausages, casings removed

2 garlic cloves, finely diced

½ teaspoon fennel seeds, crushed

½ teaspoon dried chilli flakes, crushed

800 ml (27 fl oz) passata (puréed tomatoes)

250 ml (8½ fl oz/1 cup) chicken stock

handful of basil leaves

sea salt and freshly cracked black pepper

500 g (1 lb 2 oz) dried ziti

250 g (9 oz) fresh mozzarella, thinly sliced

50 g (1¾ oz/½ cup) finely grated fresh pecorino

250 g (9 oz/1 cup) good-quality firm ricotta

Preheat the oven to 180°C (350°F). Grease a 23 cm x 33 cm (9 in x 13 in) baking dish with oil.

Heat the oil and butter in a large frying pan over medium—low heat. Add the onion and sauté for 5—7 minutes, until soft and translucent. Crumble in the sausage meat and cook for 7—9 minutes, until well-browned, then add the garlic, fennel seeds and chilli flakes and sauté for 1 minute or until fragrant. Pour in the passata and stock and simmer for 15—20 minutes, until the sauce has thickened slightly and the sausage is cooked through. Stir in the basil leaves and season to taste with salt and pepper.

Meanwhile, bring a large saucepan of salted water to the boil and cook the ziti to 1 minute less than al dente. Drain and toss the ziti through the cooked sauce.

Spoon half the ziti mixture into the baking dish and top with half the mozzarella and half the pecorino. Repeat with the remaining ziti, mozzarella and pecorino, then dollop large spoonfuls of ricotta over the top. Cover the dish with a sheet of baking paper, followed by a sheet of foil and bake for 15 minutes. Remove the foil and paper and bake for a further 15—20 minutes until the cheese has melted and the sauce is bubbling.

Allow to rest for 5 minutes before serving.

GIGLI PRIMAVERA

SERVES 4 — 6

500 g (1 lb 2 oz) dried campanelle (gigli)

150 g (5½ oz) sugar-snap peas, trimmed

150 g (5½ oz) fresh or frozen podded broad (fava) beans

150 g (5½ oz) fresh or frozen peas

30 g (1 oz) butter

1 tablespoon extra virgin olive oil

1 French shallot, finely diced

250 ml (8½ fl oz/1 cup) pure cream

250 g (9 oz) mascarpone

zest and juice of 2 lemons

freshly cracked black pepper

50 g (1¾ oz/½ cup) finely grated fresh parmesan

1 tablespoon chopped dill, plus extra sprigs to serve

1 tablespoon torn mint leaves, plus extra whole leaves to serve

sea salt

snow-pea tendrils, to serve (optional)

Bring a large saucepan of salted water to the boil and add the campanelle. When the pasta is 2 minutes less than al dente, add the sugar-snap peas and broad beans and cook for 1 minute. Add the peas and cook for a further 1 minute, then drain, reserving 60 ml (2 fl oz/¼ cup) of the pasta cooking water and set aside. Peel any larger broad beans, but leave the smaller ones whole, as they give extra texture and flavour to the dish.

Meanwhile, heat the butter and oil in a large frying pan over medium — low heat. Add the shallot and sauté for 4 minutes or until soft and translucent. Increase the heat to medium and stir through the cream, mascarpone and lemon zest and juice. Cook for 1 — 2 minutes, then season to taste with pepper.

Add the campanelle and vegetables to the creamy, lemony sauce and sprinkle over the parmesan. Stir well to combine, adding a little of the pasta water to thin the sauce, if desired. Stir through the herbs and season to taste with salt.

Divide the pasta among warm pasta bowls and garnish with the extra dill, mint and a few snow-pea tendrils (if using).

CALAMARATA WITH CALAMARI

SERVES 4 — 6

500 g (1 lb 2 oz) dried calamarata

60 ml (2 fl oz/¼ cup) extra virgin olive oil

4 garlic cloves, minced

2 tinned anchovy fillets

1 tablespoon salted baby capers, drained and rinsed

400 g (14 oz) ripe cherry tomatoes, halved

large handful of chopped parsley, plus extra to serve

3 tablespoons tomato paste (concentrated purée)

125 ml (4 fl oz/½ cup) white wine

sea salt and freshly cracked black pepper

700 g (1 lb 9 oz) small calamari hoods, cleaned and sliced into 3 cm (1¼ in) thick rings

Bring a large saucepan of salted water to the boil and cook the calamarata to 1 minute less than al dente. Drain, reserving 125 ml (4 fl oz/½ cup) of the pasta cooking water.

While the pasta is cooking, heat the oil in a large frying pan over medium — low heat. Add the garlic, anchovies and capers and sauté for 2 minutes or until fragrant. Increase the heat to medium and add the tomato halves, parsley, tomato paste and wine, stirring and tossing the ingredients together to combine. Cook for 3 — 4 minutes, then season to taste with salt and pepper.

Add the calamari to the sauce, tossing to combine, and cook for 2 — 3 minutes until the flesh is almost opaque and just cooked through. Add the calamarata and a little of the pasta water to the pan and cook everything for a further 1 — 2 minutes to allow the flavours to meld and the sauce to coat the pasta.

Divide the pasta and calamari among warm pasta bowls and serve topped with extra chopped parsley.

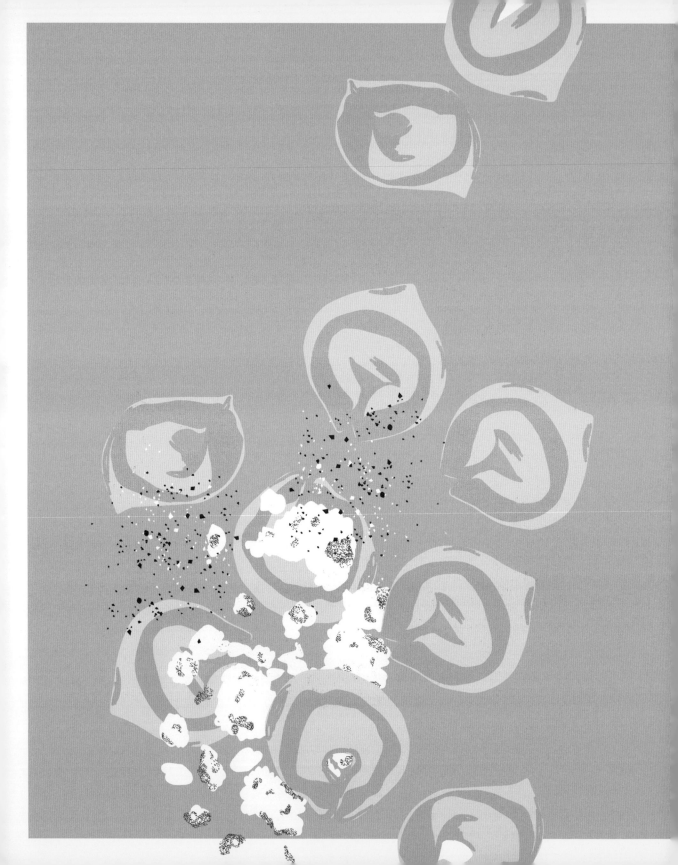

FILLED PASTA
& GNOCCHI

PROSCIUTTO, SPINACH &
RICOTTA TORTELLINI

SERVES 6 — 8

1 x quantity Egg-rich ravioli dough (see page 15)

plain (all-purpose) flour, for dusting

fine semolina flour, for dusting

1 x quantity Classic tomato sugo (see page 19)

PROSCIUTTO, SPINACH AND RICOTTA FILLING

200 g (7 oz) good-quality firm ricotta

40 g (1½ oz) parmesan, finely grated, plus extra to serve

50 g (1¾ oz) thinly sliced prosciutto, finely diced

50 g (1¾ oz) frozen spinach, thawed, squeezed dry and chopped

1 free-range egg, beaten

freshly cracked black pepper, plus extra to serve

Place the filling ingredients in the bowl of a food processor and pulse until well combined.

Roll the dough according to the instructions on page 15, then cut the dough into 6 cm (2½ in) squares using a sharp knife or pasta cutter. You should have about 80 squares of pasta.

Place 1 teaspoon of the filling in the centre of a square and moisten the edges with a little water. Fold into a triangle and seal the edges, pressing out as much air as possible to prevent air pockets, which may result in uneven cooking.

Wrap the triangle around your thumb and pinch the two points together to form a kerchief shape. Dust with plain flour, then set aside on a semolina-dusted tray and cover with a tea towel. Continue with the remaining dough and filling to make about 80 tortellini.

Bring a large saucepan of salted water to the boil and cook the tortellini in batches for 4 — 5 minutes, until al dente.

Meanwhile, heat the tomato sugo in a large saucepan over medium heat.

Using a slotted spoon, strain the tortellini into warm pasta bowls and spoon over the tomato sugo. Sprinkle with grated parmesan and pepper and serve.

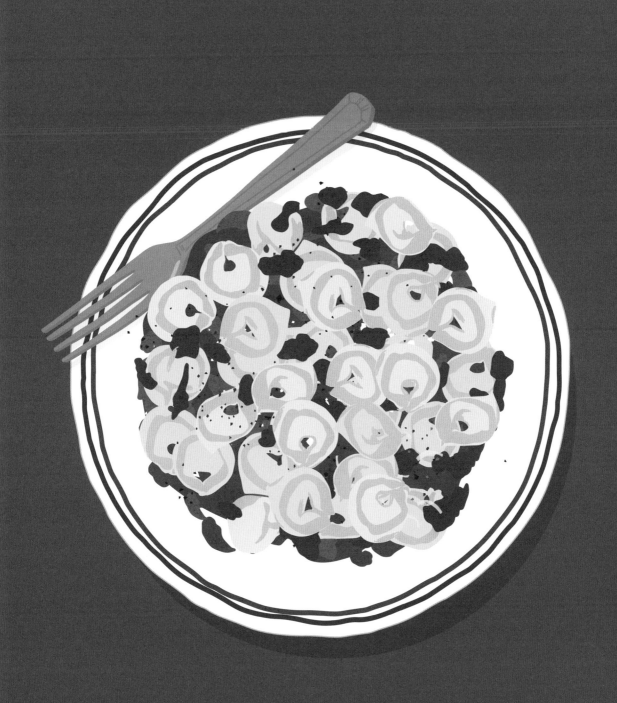

PUMPKIN RAVIOLI WITH AMARETTI & MUSTARD FRUITS IN BURNT BUTTER

SERVES 4—6

1 x quantity Egg-rich ravioli dough (see page 15)

fine semolina flour, for dusting

3—4 tablespoons mustard fruits (see Note), drained and finely diced

PUMPKIN FILLING

500 g (1 lb 2 oz) peeled and deseeded butternut pumpkin (squash), cut into 4 cm (1½ in) cubes

60 g (2 oz) good-quality sheep's milk ricotta

30 g (1 oz) parmesan, finely grated, plus extra to serve

9 small amaretti biscuits, crushed

2 teaspoons lemon zest

1 free-range egg yolk

¼ teaspoon freshly grated nutmeg

pinch of sea salt

pinch of ground white pepper

BURNT BUTTER SAUCE

200 g (7 oz) butter

30 sage leaves

sea salt and freshly cracked black pepper

To make the pumpkin filling, preheat the oven to 180°C (350°F) and line a baking tray with baking paper. Place the pumpkin on the prepared tray and roast for 45 minutes or until soft and cooked through. Set aside to cool slightly, then transfer to the bowl of a food processor and process to a purée. Add the ricotta, parmesan, one-third of the amaretti biscuits, lemon zest, egg yolk, nutmeg, salt and white pepper, and pulse until completely combined.

Make the ravioli following the instructions on page 15, then transfer to a semolina-dusted tray and cover with a tea towel.

Bring a large saucepan of salted water to the boil and cook the ravioli in batches for 7—8 minutes, until al dente.

Meanwhile, to make the burnt butter sauce, melt the butter in a large frying pan over medium heat until it begins to foam and turn a golden-brown colour. Add the sage leaves and fry for 1—2 minutes until crisp, then season with salt and pepper. Add 3 tablespoons of the pasta cooking water and swirl in the pan to emulsify and thicken the sauce.

Using a slotted spoon, strain the ravioli into warm pasta bowls and spoon over the burnt butter sauce. Top with the remaining crushed amaretti and the mustard fruits, and serve with grated parmesan on the side for sprinkling over.

NOTE:

You can purchase mustard fruits at most delicatessens and online.

SPINACH & THREE-CHEESE MANICOTTI

SERVES 4 — 6

12 dried manicotti tubes

2 teaspoons extra virgin olive oil

TOMATO SAUCE

400 g (14 oz) tin whole tomatoes

40 g (1½ oz) butter

1 tablespoon extra virgin olive oil

½ onion, finely diced

3 garlic cloves, minced

500 ml (17 fl oz/2 cups) passata
(puréed tomatoes)

½ teaspoon sugar

small handful of basil leaves

sea salt and freshly cracked
black pepper

SPINACH AND THREE-CHEESE FILLING

40 g (1½ oz) butter

1 tablespoon extra virgin olive oil

½ onion, finely diced

1 garlic clove, minced

400 g (14 oz) frozen spinach, thawed
and squeezed dry

600 g (1 lb 5 oz) firm ricotta

175 g (6 oz) freshly grated
mozzarella, plus extra to serve

160 g (5½ oz) finely grated pecorino,
plus extra to serve (optional)

1 teaspoon freshly grated nutmeg

2 free-range eggs

To make the tomato sauce, tip the tomatoes into a bowl and lightly crush them with your hands.

Heat the butter and oil in a large frying pan over medium — low heat. Add the onion and sauté for 6 — 7 minutes, until soft and translucent, then add the garlic and sauté for a further 1 minute. Stir in the tomatoes, passata, sugar and basil and cook for 15 — 20 minutes, until slightly reduced.

Meanwhile, to make the filling, heat the butter and oil in a large frying pan over medium — low heat. Add the onion and sauté for 6 — 7 minutes until soft and translucent. Add the garlic and sauté for a further 1 minute. Transfer the mixture to a large bowl and set aside to cool.

Mix the spinach, ricotta, 100 g (3½ oz) of the mozzarella, 135 g (5 oz) of the pecorino and the nutmeg into the onion mixture and season to taste with salt and pepper. Add the eggs and mix well to combine.

Bring a large saucepan of salted water to the boil and cook the manicotti to 1 minute less than al dente. Drain and refresh under cold water, then toss through the olive oil and set aside.

Preheat the oven to 180°C (350°F).

Pour half the tomato sauce into the bottom of a 33 cm x 23 cm (13¼ in x 9 in) baking dish. Use a spoon to fill the manicotti tubes with the spinach and cheese filling, then place them in the baking dish (you should have two rows of six tubes). Cover with the remaining tomato sauce and sprinkle over the remaining mozzarella and pecorino.

Cover the dish with a sheet of baking paper followed by a sheet of foil, then transfer to the oven and bake for 30 minutes.

Remove the foil and paper and bake for a further 10 minutes, or until the sauce is bubbling, the pasta is cooked through and the cheese is melted and golden. Serve warm with extra grated mozzarella and pecorino, if desired.

ZUCCHINI & KALE-STUFFED CONCHIGLIONI

SERVES 6 — 8

45 dried conchiglioni rigati

200 g (7 oz) kale leaves, sliced

80 ml (2½ fl oz/⅓ cup) extra virgin olive oil

3 zucchini (courgettes), cut into small dice

1 x quantity Vegan ricotta (see page 21)

sea salt and freshly cracked black pepper

1 x quantity Roasted tomato sugo (see page 19)

3 tablespoons Vegan pangrattato (see page 22)

Vegan parmesan (see page 21, to serve (optional)

Bring a large saucepan of salted water to the boil and cook the pasta shells to 1 minute less than al dente. Drain and refresh under cold water. Set aside.

Blanch the kale leaves for 1 — 2 minutes, then drain and refresh under cold water. Squeeze out as much liquid as possible and set aside in a large bowl.

Heat 2 tablespoons of the oil in a frying pan over medium heat. Add the zucchini and sauté for 3 — 5 minutes, until softened. Set aside to cool slightly before adding to the kale. Stir through the ricotta, season well with salt and pepper and mix well to combine.

Preheat the oven to 180°C (350°F).

Pour 750 ml (25½ fl oz/3 cups) of the tomato sugo into the bottom of a large baking dish.

Fill the conchiglioni with the vegetable ricotta mixture and nestle them together in the baking dish.

Spoon a dollop of the remaining tomato sugo over each pasta shell, sprinkle over the pangrattato and drizzle with the remaining oil. Cover the dish with a sheet of baking paper followed by a sheet of foil, then transfer to the oven and bake for 25 minutes or until lightly golden.

Serve with vegan parmesan, if desired.

PORK, FENNEL & FIOR DI LATTE-STUFFED PACCHERI

SERVES 4—6

1 x quantity Béchamel sauce (see page 20)

500 g (1 lb 2 oz) dried paccheri

200 g (7 oz) ball fior di latte, diced

freshly grated parmesan, to serve

PORK AND FENNEL RAGU

250 g (9 oz) tinned whole tomatoes

2 tablespoons extra virgin olive oil

1 large onion, finely diced

1 small fennel bulb, finely diced

3 garlic cloves, minced

½ teaspoon fennel seeds, crushed

1½ teaspoons chopped rosemary leaves

1½ teaspoons chopped oregano leaves

600 g (1 lb 5 oz) spicy Italian pork sausages, casings removed

250 ml (8½ fl oz/1 cup) red wine

375 ml (12½ fl oz/1½ cups) chicken stock

400 ml (14 fl oz) passata (puréed tomatoes)

2 fresh or dried bay leaves

sea salt and freshly cracked black pepper

small handful of parsley leaves, chopped

To make the ragu, tip the tomatoes into a bowl and lightly crush them with your hands.

Heat the oil in a large frying pan over medium heat. Add the onion and fennel and sauté for 5—7 minutes, until the onion is soft and translucent. Add the garlic, fennel seeds, rosemary and oregano and cook for 1 minute or until fragrant. Crumble in the sausage and cook, stirring, for 3—4 minutes until browned. Add the wine, increase the heat to medium—high and deglaze the pan for 2—3 minutes. Add the stock, passata, crushed tomatoes and bay leaves, then reduce the heat to medium and simmer, stirring occasionally, for 50—60 minutes, until reduced to a thick, rich sauce. Season to taste with salt and pepper and stir through the parsley.

Preheat the oven to 180°C (350°F).

Spread half the béchamel sauce over the bottom of a 25 cm (10 in) round baking dish.

Bring a large saucepan of salted water to the boil and cook the paccheri to 1 minute less than al dente. Drain and stand the pacherri upright in the baking dish. Use a small spoon to evenly fill the paccheri with the ragu and diced fior di latte, then spoon over the remaining béchamel. Transfer to the oven and bake for about 30 minutes or until golden and bubbling.

Serve with grated parmesan on the side for sprinkling over.

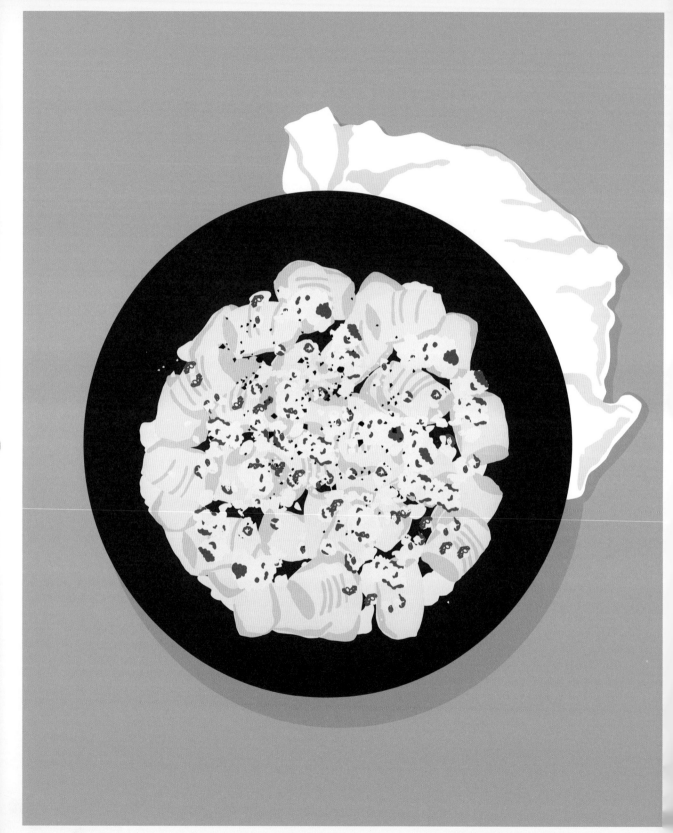

POTATO GNOCCHI WITH GORGONZOLA SAUCE

SERVES 4—6

1 x quantity cooked Potato gnocchi
(see page 18)

GORGONZOLA SAUCE

30 g (1 oz) butter

375 ml (12½ fl oz/1½ cups) pure
cream

200 g (7 oz) dolce gorgonzola or
cambozola (rind removed), diced

100 g (3½ oz) crumbly picante
gorgonzola, diced

freshly cracked black pepper

sea salt (optional)

pinch of freshly grated nutmeg
(optional)

freshly grated parmesan or extra
picante gorgonzola, crumbled, to
serve (optional)

Warm the butter and cream in a large frying pan over medium
heat, then add the cheeses and stir through.

Keep stirring the mixture until all the cheese has melted and the
ingredients meld together. Taste and season with black pepper
and add a little salt and the nutmeg, if desired. Reduce the heat to
low and cook the sauce for a further 1—2 minutes, until rich and
thick. Add the gnocchi to the pan and stir to coat in the sauce.

Divide the gnocchi among warm pasta bowls and top with freshly
grated parmesan or an extra crumble of gorgonzola, if desired.

RICOTTA GNOCCHI WITH
HERB BUTTER SAUCE

SERVES 4

460 g (1 lb) good-quality fresh ricotta, drained for 4 hours or overnight in the fridge

110 g (4 oz/¾ cup) plain (all-purpose) flour, plus extra for dusting

1 free-range egg

¼ teaspoon fine sea salt

30 g (1 oz) pecorino, finely grated, plus extra to serve

HERB BUTTER SAUCE

100 g (3½ oz) butter, cubed

large handful of mixed herbs, such as garlic chives, rosemary, sage and oregano, finely chopped

sea salt and freshly cracked black pepper

Place the ricotta, flour, egg, salt and pecorino in a large bowl. Using your hands, gently combine and bring the ingredients together. Shape into a round ball.

Divide the ball into four even portions. Dust a work surface with flour and roll each portion into a 40 cm (16 in) long rope that's 1.5 cm — 2 cm (½ in — ¾ in) wide.

Slice each rope into 20 even pieces.

Bring a large saucepan of salted water to the boil. Working in batches, cook the gnocchi for 1 — 1½ minutes, until the gnocchi rise to the top. Use a slotted spoon to transfer the gnocchi to warm pasta bowls.

Meanwhile, to make the herb butter sauce, melt the butter in a large frying pan over medium heat and toss through the herbs. Gently sauté for 1 minute, then season to taste with salt and pepper.

Pour the herb butter sauce over the gnocchi and serve topped with plenty of grated pecorino.

SILVERBEET & RICOTTA GNUDI WITH ROASTED TOMATO SUGO

SERVES 4

350 g (12½ oz) silverbeet (Swiss chard) leaves, sliced

400 g (14 oz) good-quality fresh ricotta, drained for 4 hours or overnight in the fridge

2 free-range eggs

80 g (2¾ oz) parmesan, finely grated, plus extra to serve

¼ teaspoon freshly grated nutmeg

pinch of ground allspice

¼ teaspoon fine sea salt

¼ teaspoon freshly cracked black pepper

70 g (2½ oz) plain (all-purpose) flour, plus extra for dusting

375 — 500 ml (12½ — 17 fl oz) Roasted tomato sugo (see page 19)

2 tablespoons melted butter

Bring a large saucepan of water to the boil and blanch the silverbeet leaves for 1 — 2 minutes, until wilted. Drain, refresh in iced water, then squeeze dry and finely chop. Transfer to a large bowl, add the drained ricotta, eggs, parmesan, nutmeg, allspice, salt, pepper and flour and mix well to combine.

Roll the spinach and ricotta mixture into walnut-sized balls, then roll in a dusting of flour and set aside for 30 minutes to rest.

Bring a large saucepan of salted water to the boil and, working in batches, cook the gnudi for about 4 minutes, until they rise to the surface. Use a slotted spoon to transfer the gnudi to warm pasta bowls.

Meanwhile, warm through the roasted tomato sugo. Spoon the sugo over the gnudi, drizzle over a little melted butter and serve topped with grated parmesan.

BAKED SEMOLINA GNOCCHI
(ALLA ROMANA)

SERVES 4

1 litre (34 fl oz/4 cups) full-cream (whole) milk

80 g (2¾ oz) butter

1 teaspoon fine sea salt

½ teaspoon freshly grated nutmeg, plus extra to serve

225 g (8 oz) fine semolina flour

100 g (3½ oz/1 cup) finely grated fresh parmesan

2 free-range egg yolks

freshly cracked black pepper

Place the milk, 50 g (1¾ oz) of the butter, the salt and nutmeg in a saucepan over high heat and bring to the boil. Working quickly, pour the semolina flour into the pan in a continuous stream, whisking constantly to avoid lumps forming.

Reduce the heat to medium and continue whisking for 3 — 4 minutes. As the mixture thickens, replace the whisk with a wooden spoon and continue stirring until a dough forms. Remove from the heat, add 80 g (2¾ oz) of the parmesan and stir to incorporate. Next, add the egg yolks one at a time, beating thoroughly into the mixture before adding the next.

Line a 33 cm x 23 cm (13¼ in x 9 in) baking dish with baking paper, then using a spatula, spoon and smoothly spread the semolina mixture into the dish to a depth of about 1.5 cm (½ in). Set aside for 40 — 60 minutes to completely cool and set.

Preheat the oven to 200°C (400°F).

Using a 5 cm (2 in) round pastry cutter, cut the semolina into 16 discs.

Grease a large baking dish with 2 teaspoons of the remaining butter and lay the discs in slightly overlapping rows. Dot the gnocchi with the remaining butter, sprinkle over the remaining parmesan and season with black pepper and extra nutmeg.

Bake for 20 — 25 minutes, until golden and crisp.

Divide the gnocchi among warmed plates and serve immediately.

POTATO GNOCCHI WITH CREAMY MUSHROOMS, THYME & KALE

SERVES 4—6

5 g (¼ oz) dried porcini mushrooms

60 g (2 oz) butter

60 ml (2 fl oz/¼ cup) extra virgin olive oil

1 French shallot, finely diced

5 garlic cloves, minced

500 g (1 lb 2 oz) mixed wild mushrooms, sliced

3 thyme sprigs, leaves picked and chopped

6 sage leaves, chopped

1 small rosemary sprig, leaves picked and finely chopped

125 ml (4 fl oz/½ cup) white wine

250 ml (8½ fl oz/1 cup) pure cream

sea salt and freshly cracked black pepper

70 g (2½ oz) baby kale leaves

25 g (1 oz/¼ cup) finely grated fresh parmesan, plus extra to serve

1 x quantity cooked Potato gnocchi (see page 18)

125 ml (4 fl oz/½ cup) gnocchi cooking water (optional)

lemon zest, to serve

Place the porcini mushrooms in a small bowl and cover with hot water. Leave to rehydrate for 15 minutes, then drain and finely chop. Set aside.

Heat the butter and oil in a large frying pan over medium—low heat. Add the shallot and garlic and sauté for 3—4 minutes until soft and translucent. Increase the heat to medium—high, add the mushrooms and herbs and sauté for 8—10 minutes until the mushrooms are golden. Add the wine and deglaze the pan for 2—3 minutes, then add the cream. Reduce the heat to medium and simmer, stirring occasionally, for 7—8 minutes, until the sauce is rich and thick. Season to taste with salt and pepper, then stir through the kale leaves until just wilted. Finally, stir through the parmesan.

Add the cooked gnocchi to the pan and toss to coat in the creamy mushroom sauce. Add a little of the gnocchi cooking water to thin the sauce, if desired.

Spoon the gnocchi into warm pasta bowls and serve topped with a little lemon zest and finely grated parmesan.

POTATO GNOCCHI WITH
SAUSAGE RAGU

SERVES 4—6

1 x quantity cooked Potato gnocchi
(see page 18)

SAUSAGE RAGU

60 ml (2 fl oz/¼ cup) extra virgin
olive oil

1 carrot, finely diced

1 large celery stalk, finely diced

1 red onion, finely diced

1½ teaspoons finely chopped
rosemary leaves

1½ teaspoons finely chopped
oregano leaves

600 g (1 lb 5 oz) Italian pork
sausages, casings removed

250 ml (8½ fl oz/1 cup) red wine

375 ml (12½ fl oz/1½ cups) chicken
stock

650 ml (22 fl oz) passata (puréed
tomatoes)

2 fresh or dried bay leaves

sea salt and freshly cracked
black pepper

large handful of parsley leaves,
chopped

freshly grated pecorino, to serve

To make the ragu, heat the oil in a large frying pan over medium heat. Add the carrot, celery and onion and sauté for 5—7 minutes, until the onion is translucent and the vegetables are soft. Add the herbs and cook for 1 minute or until fragrant. Crumble in the sausage and cook, stirring, for 3—4 minutes, until browned. Increase the heat to medium—high, add the wine and deglaze the pan for 2—3 minutes. Add the stock, passata and bay leaves, then reduce the heat to medium and simmer, stirring occasionally, for 50—60 minutes, until the ragu has reduced to a thick, rich sauce. Season to taste with salt and pepper and stir through half the chopped parsley.

Add the cooked gnocchi to the pan and toss to coat in the ragu. Divide the gnocchi and ragu among warm pasta bowls, sprinkle over the remaining parsley and the pecorino, and serve.

INDEX BY INGREDIENT

INDEX BY PASTA

Smith Street Books

Published in 2019 by Smith Street Books
Melbourne | Australia
smithstreetbooks.com

ISBN: 978-1-9258-1120-9

Publisher: Paul McNally
Design and art direction: Michelle Mackintosh
Recipes: Deborah Kaloper
Illustrations: Alice Oehr
Layout: Heather Menzies, Studio31 Graphics
Project manager and editor: Lucy Heaver, Tusk studio

Printed & bound in China by C&C Offset Printing
 Co., Ltd.

Book 98
10 9 8 7 6 5 4 3 2 1

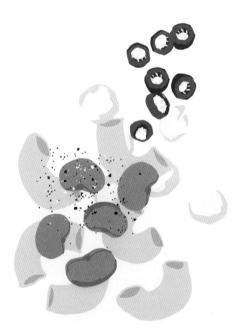

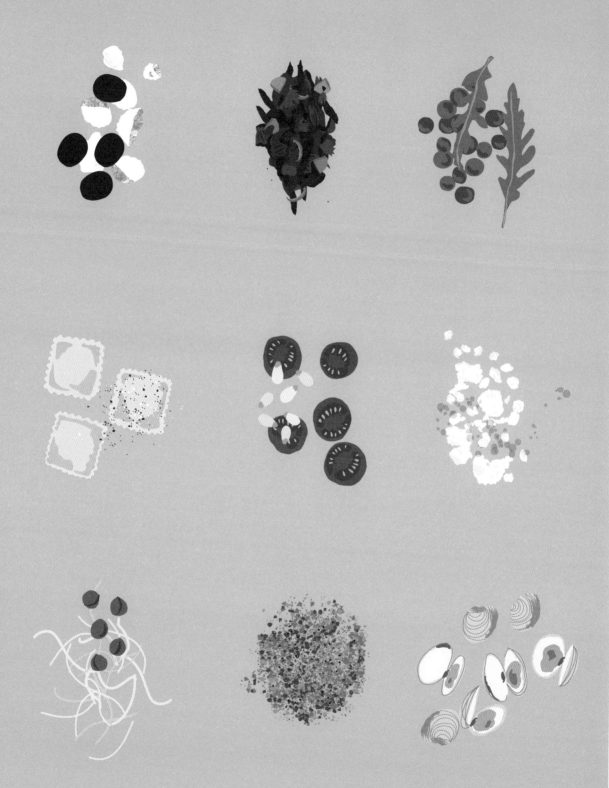

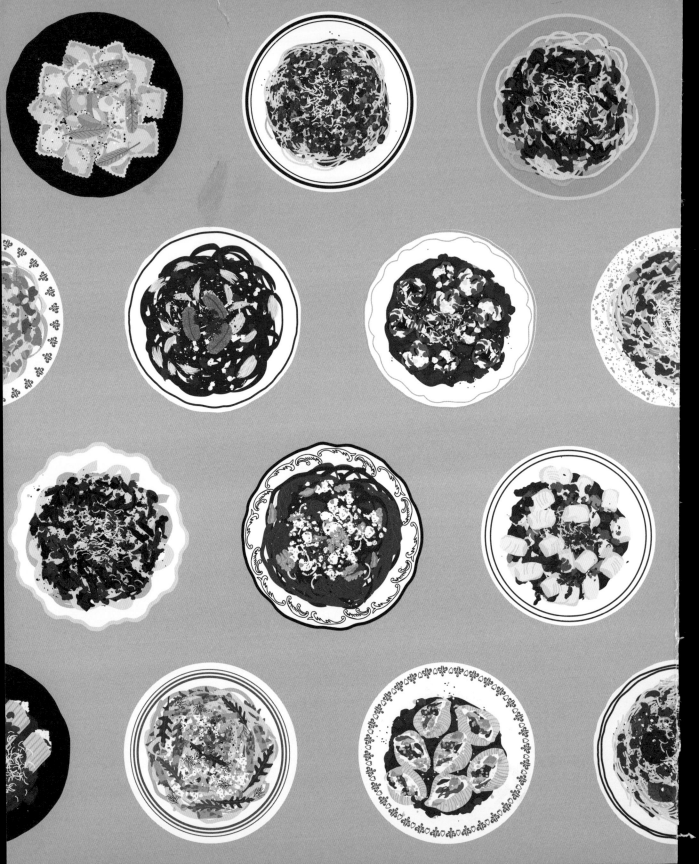